Thames & Hudson

The New Artisans II

OLIVIER DUPON

725 illustrations, 718 in color

Contents

The New Artisans II © 2015 Olivier Dupon

All Rights Reserved. No part of this publication may be reproduced or transmitted in any form or by any means, electronic or mechanical, including photocopy, recording or any other information storage and retrieval system, without prior permission in writing from the publisher.

First published in 2015 in hardcover in the United States of America by Thames & Hudson Inc., 500 Fifth Avenue, New York, New York 10110

thamesandhudsonusa.com

Library of Congress Catalog Card Number 2014944630

ISBN 978-0-500-51775-8

Printed and bound in China by C & C Offset Printing Co. Ltd

The Directory

Introduction

Craft – with a capital 'C' – is no longer a trend; it is at last enshrined in contemporary life. After the first *New Artisans* book was published in 2011 to an extremely positive reception – countless media reviews, umpteen happy readers, and the ultimate form of flattery that is having the concept and title become a major source of inspiration for others – the one question that kept popping up was: 'When are you going to do a follow-up?' The answer is in the 320 pages you hold in your hand.

This sequel results from the further pursuit and exploration of accessible but top-quality artisanship. It features sixty new names, across nineteen countries, with the intent of celebrating various forms of media – ceramics, metal, paper, textiles, wood and glass, among them – through desirable objects suited for our modern lifestyle. All sixty talents are creators I highly admire, and I would be more than happy to surround myself with their wishlist-worthy creations.

Once again, the 'handmade-with-love' ethos – also the trigger for numerous environmental and societal advantages – positions itself as the way to go. It delivers as many benefits to the maker as to the receiver, locking the two in respective gratitude. What's not to like about products that are so special one simply cannot buy multiple identical versions directly from the shelves of soulless retail stores? These are products that are tangible extensions of someone else's being. French *plumassier* Maxime Leroy (p.148) describes it best: 'My creative style is a bridge between my sensibility and my subconscious. It is a sort of prolongation of who I am…so each work ends up containing a part of me.' In an age when many experiences end up being digital, handmade offers the antithesis of virtual and becomes a necessity to reconnect with humanity.

In addition, of course, there is the politically charged topic of local supply versus remote manufacturing, which is often summarized by the biblical divide: good versus evil. Sure, it is cheaper to buy throwaway junk, but at what real cost? This important question is central to many a maker's vocation. The German duo Ina Woelk and Philipp Hinderer, aka Res Anima (p.192), have made a motto out of the comment supposedly made by John Ruskin: 'I am too poor to afford cheap goods.'

Moreover, the fact that one can often meet and talk with the makers directly offers a unique opportunity to negotiate a bespoke project that suits one's budget, as Australian wood wizard Greg Hatton (p.76) suggests: 'If someone comes to me and expresses their passion for a piece, I will give them options on materials that have a range in prices or, worst-case scenario,' he quips, 'I'll teach them how to make it themselves!'

This generous streak – the will to share their craft – is present in all the makers interviewed for the *New Artisans* books. Take Chilean embroiderer *extraordinaire*, Karen Barbé (p.108), who is already 'teaching embroidery techniques in a contemporary language aimed at designers, makers, artists and illustrators'. She also wants to research and collect 'productive experiences, in order to build solid working activities around craft; a way to tackle the conception that craftsmen struggle to make a living out of their creations and to attract younger generations towards this kind of career path'.

Artisanship is a precursor and part of what is now known as 'Slow Design', the holistic approach to creation. What we eat, wear and buy defines who we are. So, more than ever, supporting local traders and buying their ingeniously handcrafted pieces seems common sense at the very least. British artist Rosemary Milner (p.196) believes that people are now more enthusiastic about the 'make do and mend' philosophy and more willing to get involved. 'The population is reverting back to the age-old traditions and is investing in objects that will last a lifetime. There are also a lot more skills being practised through workshops so people can create beautiful objects themselves. In the Victorian and Georgian periods, a lady would never have strayed far without a needle and thread: I believe we are going back to this way of thinking and appreciating bespoke objects rather than mass-produced commodities.'

One of the many perks of working on a project like *The New Artisans* is the chance to share the life-stories and commitment of makers from all over the world. Whenever and wherever I am able to travel, I look out for their pieces in galleries or shops, and this always brings back memories of inspirational and enjoyable encounters.

Charming artisans such as Japanese maker Takashi Tomii (p.220) credit handmaking as a key source of happiness: 'I view craft as simple, beautiful and essential in my life. I am surrounded by my work, as well as by many other craftsmen's pieces from now and the past,' he says. 'The work never feels like routine because I always try to make things better, even when I'm making the same series. It's always challenging – but oh so rewarding – to create the simplest utensils with something of the "sublime" in them.'

On that aspirational note, I hope you enjoy discovering the artisans within this volume. Like Takashi, they all have enchanting tales to tell and with the same delight and hope in our collective future as I share myself.

Abigail Brown

UK

They are the sort of handcrafted wonders that make children's eyes sparkle…and grown-ups' as well. Abigail Brown's avian textile sculptures – an ornithologist's fantasy – include flamingos, woodpeckers, herons… You name it, Abigail has replicated it, mainly with pre-used fabrics, recycling her old clothes and asking friends and colleagues for remnants. 'I decide on a piece, then start researching on the internet, pulling photos of the bird from all angles so that these can inform the drawing I make to create the template,' explains Abigail. 'I sew the body, inserting a wire piece to form the beak and legs, then I stuff it tightly, shaping as I go.' Abigail selects fabrics to get the closest possible match to the bird's plumage. 'I cut and stick, working from the tail, covering the body in small pieces of fabric. The final stage is to sew in the detail in black thread. These tiny stitches hold the fabric, in addition to glue, but they are mostly there for decoration. When the eyes are in place, the piece finally comes to life – a very satisfying moment.' Although, in the seven years since she started, Abigail's style has evolved from childlike and illustrative to more sophisticated and realistic, she has kept the black stitching as a trademark, and her flair for strong colours

remains intact. Having been inspired by her seamstress grandmother, Abigail went on to do a degree in surface decoration and printed textiles, but she didn't feel she had found herself until a friend introduced her to the world of decorative artefacts. 'All this work that I make now is a process of discovery: all self-taught and a case of trial and error.' Years spent freelancing as an illustrator, then as a designer of greetings cards, stationery and children's clothing, then as a designer at a children's book publisher have informed her proficiency at visual expression. Entering her London workshop is like stepping into a vibrant sanctuary. Her exotic birds and native species alike are literally therapeutic. 'A counsellor working with people who had suffered domestic abuse bought them in flocks before explaining where they were going. My birds encouraged small children to voice what they weren't able to say themselves,' Abigail notes with gratitude. 'Every day should be full of happiness, magic and wonder. Just as a smile is contagious, so inspiring thoughts brought to life inspire others.' A sentiment that should be proclaimed across the world.

See also p.308
www.abigail-brown.co.uk

5

6

11

7

5. Everywhere one looks in Abigail's workshop, birds preside over the making of their future companions.

6. Tropicana emanates from this still life, whose exotic stars are a peach-faced lovebird and a Bourke's parakeet.

7. The workshop-turned-aviary features a ringed teal, a pheasant, a greater spotted woodpecker and a little ringed plover.

3. A heron stands on the mantelpiece. Is he 'preying' for fish?

4. Abigail's vibrant décor provides ideal spots for birds to perch: here a Gurney's Pitta and a grey-headed kingfisher.

1. Abigail Brown sewing a duck with surgical precision.

2. Tweet, tweet! A fabric blue tit and chaffinch.

Amy Jayne Hughes

UK

You know you have accomplished something when a connoisseur such as Tricia Guild, founder of Designers Guild, describes you as a 'superior ceramicist' and your work as 'extraordinary'; when the *Sunday Times* mentions you alongside Barber Osgerby and says you are 'tipped for greatness'; and when a Parisian collector displays one of your pieces next to his Picasso. The deserving recipient of all these accolades is British ceramicist, Amy Jayne Hughes. Ironically, she notes, 'I am not from a particularly artistic family and art practice was never massively encouraged at school; it was just something I always did in one form or another. Later, an incredible teacher, Warren Dunn, prompted me to take the path that has led me to where I am today.' Various temping jobs, including working in an accounts department and filing hospital medical records, only strengthened Amy Jayne's resolve. 'I decided to opt for a foundation diploma in art to find out exactly which bit it was that drove me. I had never done any ceramics before and thought the idea ridiculous, but nine years on I am still practising it,' she laughs. 'My work has been through huge changes in that time, especially during my Masters at the Royal College of Art. I would say it has become more sculptural and

textured, and more about the material from which it is made.' Amy Jayne now shares a studio with eight former RCA classmates, who have collectively transformed a railway arch under the East London line into a multidisciplinary art and design studio, known as Manifold. Of her own collections, she explains, 'They aim to bridge the gap between the past and the present.' Contrasting the highly refined, densely decorated porcelain *objets d'art* produced at the Royal Sèvres factory in the late 17th and 18th centuries, she notes that her own pieces feature free-floating illustrations done in an observational style, with a loosely held pen and painterly washes of colour. 'I find this way you can truly capture the qualities and characteristics of your subject.' The materiality of the clay is elevated and celebrated, each piece establishing a fresh dialogue between form and decoration. Of her now recognizable vases, she says, 'I hand-build, combining coiling, press-moulding and sprigging techniques.' In embracing innovation, while maintaining nods to familiar references, Amy Jayne is well equipped to take the world of ceramics by storm.

See also p.256
www.amyjaynehughes.com

1. Amy Jayne Hughes using a wooden modelling tool to put the finishing touches to the rim of a raw vase.

2. Detail of one of two plates from the 'Nouveau Bleu Platter' series.

3. Homage to London: 'Tower Bridge', part of the 'Landmarks' series.

4. Fit for a king's table: 'A Wash with Couleur', from the 'Full Tableware' collection.

3

4

1. Ana Hagopian's most important 'tools' are her hands.

2. The 'Snake' necklace, smoothly undulating in folded paper.

3, 4. Ana's home is also her creative den. Old floorboards, huge French windows and original architectural details combine to make a beautiful canvas for her poetic compositions.

5. Like a mellifluous sound: the 'Curly' necklace, made using a mix of techniques.

5

6. Echoing the fading beauty of flowers: 'Liana Tween', mixed techniques.

7. The 'Blueberries' necklace, in mixed techniques, is delicious to the eye.

8. The 'Seeds' necklace in vibrant papier-mâché.

19

Anne Léger

Norway

Things are always off to a good start once Anne Léger has foraged enough elements with the potential to come together to form a single sculptural piece of jewelry, each embodying an underlying storyline. Under Anne's watchful eye, Japanese wood, sterling silver, enamel, copper, pearls, gemstones and, from time to time, alchemical oddities such as her son's milk teeth, tears, gun cartridges and circular saw blades are layered until the whole becomes greater than the sum of its parts. Anne's studio is self-admittedly chaotic, for it reflects her need to be surrounded by the collected components she might need for a future piece. 'My curiosity, my ability to experiment and my sensibility for composition allow me to take advantage of an intuitive process that leads my way in the creative process. At the very start I don't have a precise idea of how the final result will work or what it will look like; I just have an idea about a feeling I want to express. So I create several elements in different forms or colours and begin to associate these together,' she explains. 'When the composition seems to take the form I wish, I add or withdraw elements until it reaches the balance I am searching for. It's an ongoing dialectic process. One thing I cannot control, though, is enamel. It has a

frightening, fascinating will of its own!' The strong sense of visual orchestration in Anne's work can no doubt be explained by the Masters in photography she obtained in France, followed by the Masters in metal and jewelry-making she received after moving to Oslo, where she now lives. Each of her adornments has a timeless flamboyance – the kind celebrated in legends, in which necklaces resemble talismanic breastplates and jewelry is above all incantatory. 'There's a strong emphasis on detail in my pieces, and sometimes they play with their own mythology,' she states. Her botanical and ornamental elements are often inspired by Art Nouveau motifs, while her narrative tableaux draw on stylized and abstract images. 'Nature, René Lalique, Charles Baudelaire, the movie *In the Mood for Love*, my interpretation of Japan, Boris Vian, French singer Barbara and random anecdotes all inspire me. But I have to make sure I don't repeat myself.' Finally, she adds, holding the functional and conceptual in perfect balance: 'The full meaning and content of my creations can only be revealed by the individuality of the person wearing them.'

See also p.273
www.anneleger.com

Anne Léger filing the sharp edge of a silver frame to be incorporated in the reverse of a wooden brooch.

3. As much an artwork as a piece of jewelry: the 'Chrysanthème' brooch in wood, silver, enamel and steel.

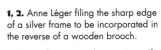
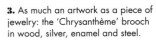

21

1. Aude Tahon making a 'ginger' knot with two lengths of cotton thread and an awl.

2. An assortment of old and new ginger knot swatches, which Aude keeps for colour and pattern reference.

3. 'Robe Cocon' – a dress made of wax-resist dyed and pleated abaca fibres in a network of gimped silk knots, using the Korean knots technique – commissioned and acquired by the Musée des Tissus in Lyon.

4. 'Veste Ossature': a jacket in wax-resist dyed abaca fibres in a network of gimped silk knots, made using the Korean knots technique.

5. Aude's treasure trove of silk and cotton thread spools.

6. Self-portrait of the artist wearing her 'Snowflake' headpiece, made with an endless knot of cotton thread and small silk tufts.

7. 'Souliers Vestige': fragile, ghostly shoes in porcelain with *mishima* surface decoration and tied thread in the Korean knots technique.

8. The 'Éventail' (Fan) necklace, showing Aude's predilection for knotting with continuous strands of yarn. The complete necklace features lotus, wing-shaped and overlapped slipknots in dyed, then painted silk-wrapped thread.

Bee Kingdom

Canada

Attending a Bee Kingdom exhibition is like stepping into an enchanted glass wonderland: ripples of saturated colour, soothing curvaceous forms, glistening surfaces and gentle creatures galore. It is digital world, *kawaii* and hyped-up beauty rolled into one, as if the Murano tradition had had a makeover through the prism of a futuristic form of pop art. The practice consists of Phillip Bandura, Tim Belliveau and Ryan Marsh Fairweather. 'Our collective workshop is in a bungalow in a quiet neighbourhood just north of downtown Calgary. The master bedroom is a three-person office, the garage is the hot glass studio, and we have a number of rooms for storage of finished commissions, works in progress and exhibition archives, as well as space to photo-shoot our sculptures.' This all-inclusive hive hosts the trio, who met at Alberta College of Art and Design, where they each received a BFA with a major in glass. The studio was in fact Phillip's family's home, which the friends rented, initially transforming it into their live/work space. 'We had so many challenges in terms of money and construction,' recalls Tim. 'When Ryan and Phil managed to turn on the flame for our glass furnace for the first time, it felt like we had done something impossible.' The studio members no longer live in the house, and ultimately the team's goal is to find a public studio with attached gallery space. For now, Phillip is involved with social rights activism ('a lot of my work has political content as part of its meaning,' he notes, often incorporating glass and other materials in interesting ways); Tim works as an illustrator specializing in graphic ink drawing (of his glass work he says, 'I make creatures and semi-narrative images, attempting to create icons for the borders between civilization and wilderness'); and Ryan teaches yoga (his glasswork is rooted in '"cute" culture, yogic philosophy and character design', often using sandblasting as the final sweet touch). 'The process of glassblowing is the draw for me,' he adds. 'When I nail a complicated or large design, it's very satisfying.' Phillip loves the fact that working with his hands allows him to think: 'The process of envisioning a work of art and then being able to make it is exhilarating.' Also vital is emphasizing teamwork. 'The idea of collaboration is the approach and meaning in a lot of the group works.' Alluring glass sculptures – charm offensives on steroids – are the happy result.

See also p.271
www.beekingdom.ca

1. Tim Belliveau using a MAP (mixed acetylene/propane) gas torch to heat a spot on a blown glass bubble, ready for sculpting.

2. Rods of 'colour bar': solid colour made of clear glass pre-melted in a factory and tinted with metals and minerals. Bee Kingdom buys these and chops them into little slices that can be warmed up on the end of a pipe and blown into a bubble of uniform tone.

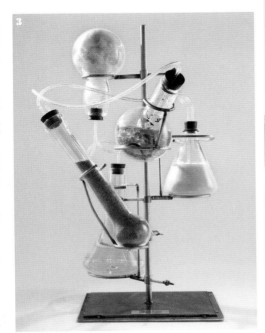

A **supercute** is a unit of cuteness equal to one and a half million kittens dressed in plush dinosaur costumes.

3. The members of Bee Kingdom love to experiment with mixed media. This piece, by Phillip Bandura, is called 'Freedomco: Home Oil Refinery Kit'.

4. 'Animated Landscape (Living Hills)' by Tim Belliveau.

5. An installation view of the 'Supercute' exhibition held at Ruberto-Ostberg Gallery, Calgary, in 2013.

6. Teamwork in action: Tim (centre) is the 'gaffer' or director of this piece. Phillip (right) brings over a hot glass 'bit' on a separate pipe to be stuck to the main piece and in due course to form a handle. Ryan Marsh Fairweather (left) uses a 'tiger torch' to warm the end of the first glass piece and keep it from cracking.

7. A modern version of Noah's Ark?
The 'Habitat Rocket (Wolf)' by Phillip
Bandura, mixed media.

8. 'Animated Landscape (Whales +
Mountains)' by Tim Belliveau, glass
and wood.

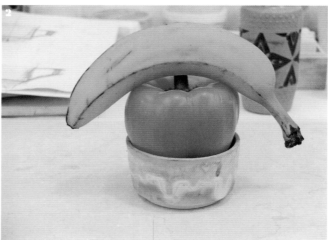

32

Ben Fiess

USA

Could it be the pastels mixed with neons that evoke bonbon jars? Or the fluoro rubber bands that indicate a playful pot that might just contain a little preserved delicacy? If the concept of 'yummy' could translate into an object, it would be into one of Ben Fiess's porcelain vessels. And, like confectionery, Ben's 'Jar' series is addictive. 'The biggest compliment I've been paid is when my undergraduate professor, Charlie Olson, offered to trade work with me.' Ben's training was in ceramic sculpture, 'so my venture into small-run-production products is new to me, and I'm finding it very rewarding'. He approaches every project holistically, paying attention to the tiniest detail. 'Porcelain sounds amazing: it's vitreous and tends to resonate clearly, rather than making thuds like non-vitreous earthenware,' he notes. 'Every project is different, and I love the opportunity to keep variety in my work. If I need to learn a new skill to complete an idea, I will gladly do so. My metalsmithing professor once gave me a card with the Helen Hayes quote, "If you rest, you rust."' Having followed in the footsteps of his parents, who are both makers, Ben has seen his work develop and flourish. 'I now appreciate the quality of clay more: it can bend, rip, crack, lump, and so on. I also include

many more colours and surfaces. It's a matter of learning the chemistry and doing experiments.' Coupling ceramic elements with other materials, such as cork and even on occasion 'fabric from clothes I've retired from my wardrobe', Ben selects the binder between the multiple stackable pieces that fit together to complete a composition. He also likes to use speckled surface effects, which some now consider to be his signature. That such modern pieces – ideal for urban interior décors – are produced in the countryside compels an extra 'Ah!' moment. Ben lives and works on a farm in rural Minnesota. 'I have studio space in a couple of rooms in the main house and my kilns are in one of the outbuildings. It's a great place to work.' He has never forgotten the words of a visiting ceramics professor, Chris Staley: 'Notice what you notice.' 'It's simple advice, but since then I've been much more cognizant of the visual cues I'm excited by. For example, one day I noticed a bright orange soccer net draped across dew-covered green grass, and the combination of colours, patterns, shapes and visual weight really struck me.' Anyone gazing at Ben's uplifting works will feel the same.

See also p.296
www.bfiess.com

3. Awaiting corks and elastic bands, this group of jars displays myriad possible colour combinations.

4. Porcelain colour samples (not suitable for playing marbles!).

5. Peekaboo: works in progress in the process of being unveiled.

1. Ben Fiess, a maker fascinated by the connections between design and composition.

2. A temporary exercise in composition: natural shapes come in handy.

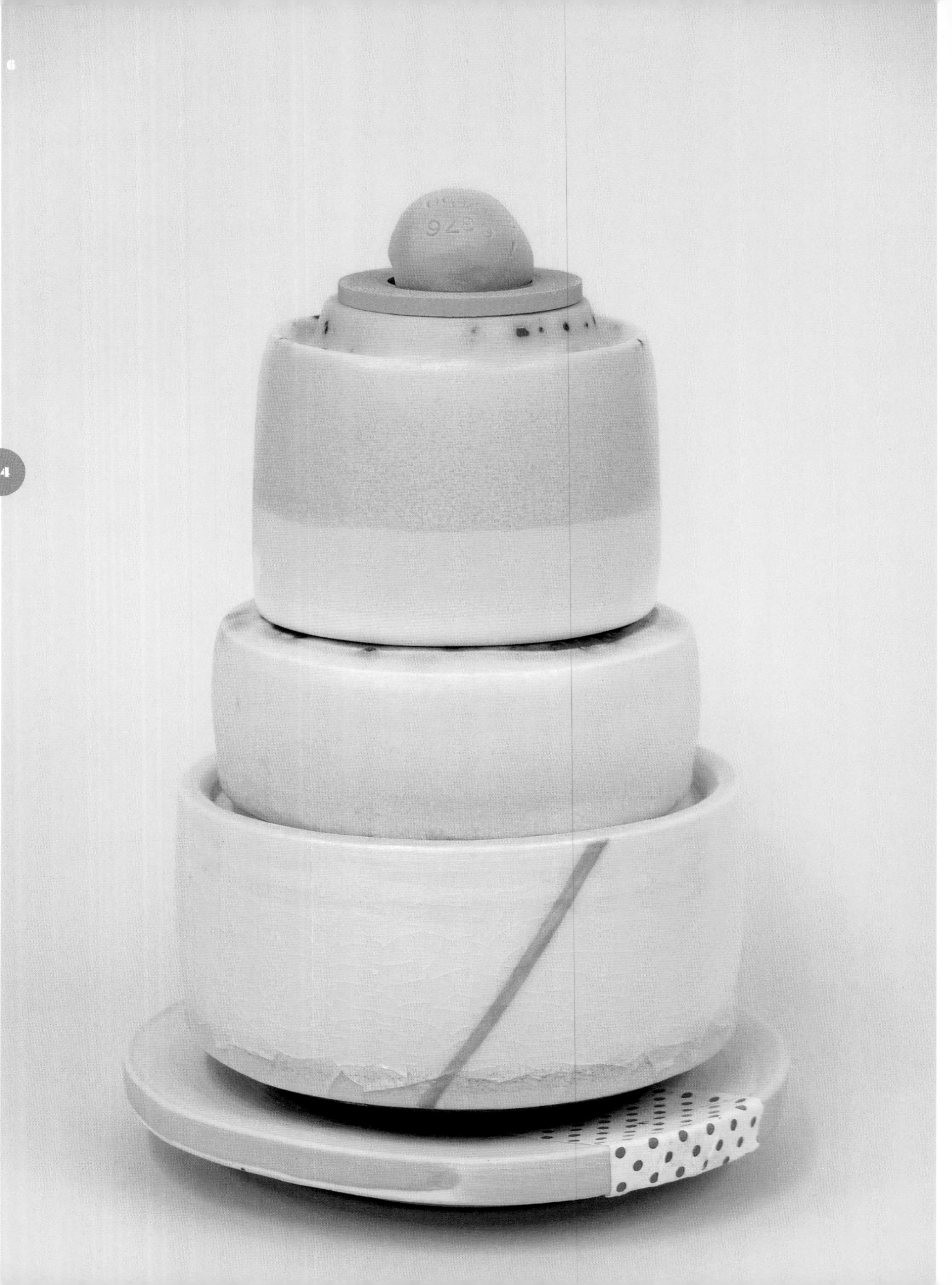

6

9, 10. Bracelets, in the 'Paper Flowers' series, made of embossed sterling silver and hand-cut anodized titanium.

11. A proud legacy: busts of Bethamy's great-grandfather, grandfather and father, all Western Australian silversmiths, sculpted by grandfather James Alexander Barrow Linton.

9

10

Brothers Dressler

Canada

Their résumé sums it up: 'Jason and Lars Dressler are twin engineers-turned-designers and material manipulators working collaboratively as Brothers Dressler.' Both attended the University of Toronto, Jason studying mechanical engineering and Lars chemical engineering. After graduating, the pair played professional basketball in Europe, Lars crediting sports with helping him to develop hand control and dexterity. Later, while working as an engineer, Jason witnessed a distinct lack of communication between the designers and the makers on the shop floor 'who knew how things actually went together: this frustrated me and motivated me to work to change that relationship'. Furthermore, when he later worked in props and set-building, he was confronted by the 'indecent waste of materials in the name of quick and profitable production of commercials and movies'. This prompted him to apprentice under skilled cabinetmakers and woodworkers, and to enrol in the craft and furniture design course at Sheridan College. When he graduated, the twins founded Brothers Dressler, 'building a few of our own designs as well as kitchens, millwork and furniture for architects, all of which gave us the confidence and experience to pursue our own work'. Their determination and work ethic, paired with a

'think out of the box' attitude, have propelled them to the forefront of the Canadian design scene. They have built a reputation for creating highly original, timeless furniture with a focus on craftsmanship and process. Some themes recur, such as natural colour gradations, repeated elements, steam-bent pieces and use of waste. 'Lars and I discuss each project and establish a first iteration,' Jason explains. 'Usually one of us takes it further before I bring it to the computer to draw it in scale. Further explorations, manipulations and prototypes are made. Designs are then built by us and our small team of talented craftspeople.' The brothers are notably keen to work responsibly. 'We source material from Toronto's urban wood and we use old-growth hardwoods from the bottom of the Great Lakes, salvaged timbers from old factories or barns, and found objects that could be from anywhere, including the garbage.' Creativity lies at the heart of everything they do. 'There is so much fulfilment in the act of creation and the pursuit of beauty. It's a worthy pursuit if it's done with the right intentions and a respect for all that it affects.'

See also pp. 266, 282
www.brothersdressler.com

1. Jason Dressler cutting a template at the Brothers Dressler lab.

2. A detail of an award-winning storefront for Lululemon in Yorkdale: a mosaic crafted from 35,788 wooden blocks made from a variety of woods salvaged from the Brothers Dressler workshop. The pixelated palette, inspired by the brothers' photograph of a fallen leaf, is comprised of all the natural colours of the woods.

43

3. A glimpse into a lofty corner of the main studio, containing finished work, experiments and objects of inspiration.

4, 5. A view of the sculptural pergola structure built for the Drake One Fifty restaurant in downtown Toronto, conceived by Martin Brudnizki; and a close look at Kai Kristiansen's beautiful joinery work supporting a submerged bent maple post and a worm-ridden maple barn beam.

6. Lars and Jason working together on preparing ash wood elements for steam-bending, part of their 'Branches' shelving system.

Catarina Riccabona

UK

At a time when most fabrics are industrially made, it is one of today's ultimate luxuries to buy from an independent artisan who is hand-weaving yarns to create unique, timeless accessories and homewares. These, of course, come with a high price tag, but one that still does not reflect the time and energy necessary to weave a single piece. Catarina Riccabona is a London-based weaver *extraordinaire*, who appears to be all set for a long-lasting career. 'I tend to work quite spontaneously,' she says. 'I like to respond to what I see is happening on the loom. Having said that, weaving requires a great deal of planning and a lot of attention, as one little mistake can ruin everything. Weaving very regularly, I feel I have certain ideas at hand, like a sort of vocabulary that I can use and combine again and again.' Her vision for the finished product is usually clear, but she also values flexibility. 'It has happened that I've decided to change the intended use: for example, I cut up a throw, once I saw the whole piece off the loom, and made it into cushions.' A highly visual person, Catarina excels at recognizing patterns and arrangements, and this could explain why block-threading is one of her favourite methods. 'When you set up the loom, you determine groups of threads that

behave in a certain way. During weaving you can either make all the blocks look the same or you can juxtapose them by using different weave structures in different blocks. I like to "compose" a fabric surface,' she notes. Her work is characterized by the material qualities of her yarns and by her soft, muted colours. 'I like it when things look a bit "unfinished" or "unprecise". I love linen for its understated elegance, the way it ages, its reliability, its relative eco-friendliness and sustainability. I avoid buying industrially or chemically dyed and bleached yarns. Instead I use second-hand yarns, both donated and from my own old stock.' She sources natural alpaca, which comes in subtle fleece colours, and buys plant-dyed Finnsheep wool from an expert in botanical dyes who grows and forages her own materials – a collaboration in line with Catarina's strong environmental credentials. This recipient of the prestigious Cockpit Arts/Clothworkers' Foundation Award muses, 'As a weaver, I am part of a cultural activity that is universal and reaches far into the past'…and surely far into the future.

See also p.312
www.catarinariccabona.com

3. Working at Loom I, with bright natural light pouring over the studio.

4. Placing the yarn spool into Shuttle II.

5. A display of works at the Cockpit Arts Open Studio in London.

1. Catarina Riccabona making some delicate adjustments at Loom III.

2. The minimalist elegance of a black and grey modernist pattern: a detail of a handwoven linen and alpaca throw.

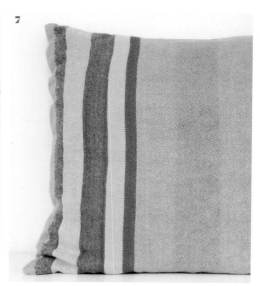

6. Catarina moving the lease sticks back for even warp tension.

7. A timeless handwoven linen cushion, featuring second-hand wool.

8. A detail of a handwoven linen and wool throw.

9. An uneven distribution of stripes and colours is a token of uniqueness in all Catarina's work, including this handwoven linen and wool throw.

10. Ready for setting up: a linen warp faces its future at the rear of the loom.

11. One for every room: handwoven linen and wool throws resting on a linen cushion.

Cathy Miles

UK

Cathy Miles dreams wire sculptures out of thin air. In her mind's eye she projects everyday observations taken from both human and natural worlds, then ingeniously articulates hollowed-out renditions that sometimes appear like intricate holograms. 'I usually start with 2D drawings. I use an ink pen in different thicknesses, as I'm trying to illustrate my findings through line,' she explains. 'Although the drawings are not an accurate representation of what will be made in wire, they get my eyes warmed up. I then dive in and start "drawing", as it were, in wire with my pliers and cutters.' Cathy sometimes includes found objects to add character, or she sends her pieces to a powder coater then paints over the top in cold enamel to add colour. She has been experimenting with model-making since art college, where she would often find wire lying around in workshops. 'Wire allows ultimate flexibility. It's good for working spontaneously, and it makes me really look and get to know my subject in depth.' In addition, she notes, 'My making allows me to discover worlds I would never otherwise have access to. Through sharing my skills I get to meet a wide variety of people and hear their stories.' Cathy admits that she needs social interaction to generate ideas,

'and I like living in a place where other makers are nearby: peer-to-peer support is very useful'. Having studied silversmithing and jewelry design in London, she assumed she would have to give up her crafting for a 'proper job'. However, her graduation show led to an exhibition offer, 'and that gave me a reason to continue and to look for other opportunities'. She won a Craft Council placement in Liverpool, and has now been working with wire for some fourteen years. In that time her work has developed in intricacy and become more experimental with colour, finishes and scale, going from as small as a honey bee to as large as a 60 cm (24 in.) teapot. 'I've also become interested in addressing the relationship between 2D and 3D, and in creating imaginary physical worlds; an entire environment in wire that the visitor can explore.' Touched by viewers' responses, such as the museum guard who instantly recognized her 'Supersize Minton Coffee Pot' and began to share his love of the pattern and tales of his time as a Minton rep, Cathy concludes, 'I love it when a piece opens up a conversation. The mundane is a delight to me.'

See also p.291
www.cathymiles.com

1. We would also be beaming if we were in Cathy Miles's workshop: a work-in-progress vase looks very promising.

2. 'Pigeons', a wire sculpture incorporating found materials, from the 'Common Bird Life' series.

3. Exotic paradise, here we come: a flock of parakeets, cockatiels and budgerigars from the 'Common Bird Life' series waits to take off.

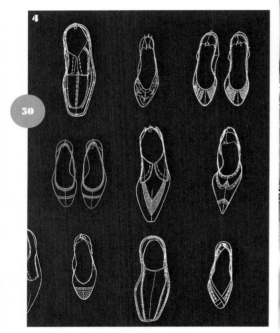

4. Shoe lovers rejoice: a glimpse of '40 shoes', a collection of wire shoe sculptures.

5. An exquisite 'Blue Ginger Jar', a painted wire sculpture from the 'Wire Vessel' collection.

6. Cathy spot-welding the joins of a decorative wire vase.

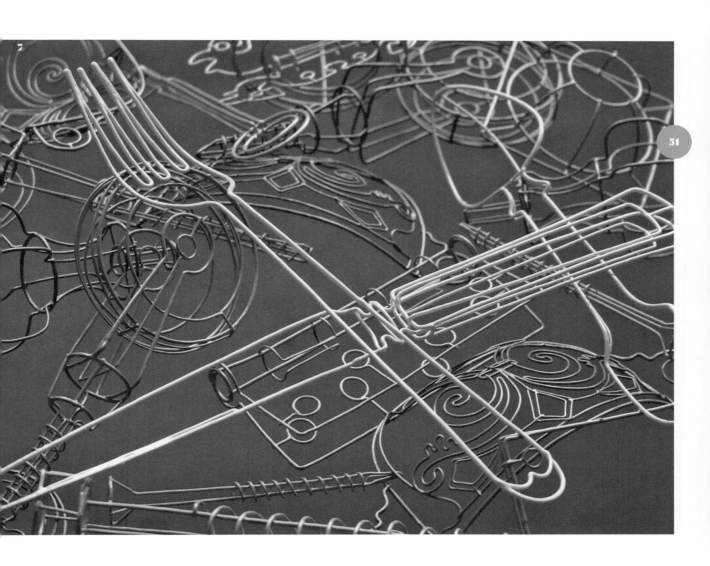

7

Claydies

Denmark

Ceramic creations from Claydies are possibly the most playful and humorous you will ever find… yet they are part of a vision that is extremely serious when it comes to concept and quality. Fan letters arrive – often from Japanese clients, ceramic connoisseurs *par excellence* – crediting Tine Broksø and Karen Kjældgård-Larsen, the duo behind the brand, for bringing joy and wit to an area of design that is often austere, and also praising them for their commitment to superior handcraft. The pair work seamlessly, from brainstorming to finishing. 'We throw tons of ideas at each other and then wait for a reaction. That way we can easily throw away ideas that don't work, because we have to agree on a concept,' the pair explain. 'We then start drafting – a little bit of drawing, but mainly making actual-size models in clay. Once we know what to make, we delegate tasks according to who has the best skills in the different fields.' Inspired by history and by old craft methods, the pair also search for elements that are far removed from the world of ceramics. 'It's a method we use a lot to try and find new ideas.' Karen enjoys throwing ('I like that it's a fast process, with a very "ceramic" expression'), while Tine prefers to hand-build ('I like to work precisely, looking

at the object again and again and optimizing the shape'). Even though their work encapsulates cleverly irreverent ideas, it is always functional. 'In our working process anything is possible, but we really like rules. This makes it natural for us to work with a common expression, even though we are two different people.' Their projects have included a show at a gallery in Copenhagen, during which they trotted on a catwalk wearing ceramic bowls inspired by hairstyles – 'a very thrilling experience!' – and a cutting-edge 'Dogma' challenge that meant they had to work blindfolded. Their work now forms part of many prestigious collections, but their ultimate wish is to democratize handmade ceramics. 'People think they can't afford to pay hundreds of kroner for a cup, but it's a question of priorities. When it comes to a pair of designer jeans that won't even last as long, they don't bat an eye and pay a fortune! We believe we have to be better at communicating the immense amount of work that goes into making just one cup.' Our inner children and our mature selves look forward to Claydies' future projects with delighted anticipation.

See also p.302
www.claydies.dk

1. Karen Kjældgård-Larsen and Tine Broksø in their workshop, discussing the outcome of a batch of ceramic jugs.

2. Most Claydies pieces have a playful, 'it's not what it seems' quality: here, the duo are wearing 'Smile' necklaces, featuring porcelain teeth, from their 'This is not a joke' collection.

3, 4. Food for thought: the 'Billy' hand-modelled stoneware hairstyle bowl, from the 'Claydies and Gentlemen' collection, presented on Tine's head and on its own.

5, 6. The 'Sally' stoneware hairstyle bowl, this time modelled by Karen.

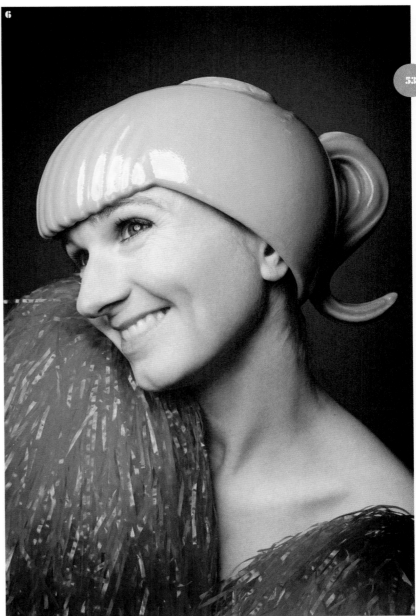

53

54

8

7. The entire, eclectic 'This is not a joke' collection – proof of the duo's unbridled imagination.

8. Karen throwing a ceramic piece on the wheel in the workshop.

9. A four-handed enterprise: Karen and Tine experimenting with new ideas.

10. Playing things by ear: hand-modelled porcelain 'Bloom' flowers attached to rubber ear syringes.

10

Clémentine Dupré

France

Smooth surfaces are studded with organic eruptions of egg- and tentacle-shaped masses. Delicate formations appear, reminiscent of a cellular organism in all its creeping beauty. However, there is no parasitic malevolence here; only a symbiotic accord between a porcelain host and its preternatural excrescences. Clémentine Dupré, the creator of these otherworldly, sensual vessels, has been operating out of a Parisian atelier for the last six years. 'The "Micro-organisme" series is a 3D fantasized version of my fascination for the swarm of human life and the organization of systems,' she explains. 'For any project, I like to start by using my imagination – a calm source of energy that shifts to a more intense involvement once I delve into the actual work. One needs patience: sometimes I have an idea and a year will pass before the actual piece is finalized. Ultimately, I am driven by the study of the dynamics between Eros and Thanatos: cycles of construction and deconstruction using architectural typologies, principles and combinatorial approaches.' In order to fulfil her dreams, Clémentine dropped a promising career as a political anthropologist to enrol in the Métiers d'Art curriculum at the École Supérieure des Arts Appliqués Duperré. She took the decision after a pivotal encounter on a field trip to China. 'Out of the blue, I decided to visit a porcelain workshop. I will never forget the moment I saw this Chinese potter throwing porcelain. I froze and stared. It was as if everything fell into place; I instantly knew I had to work with porcelain.' Clémentine has maintained her love for travel and immersion in other cultures, notably in Africa, China and Japan, where she spends a lot of time getting inspiration for her work, which often marries her interests in art, craft and anthropology. Current creative impulses include piling, building and composing structures in the 'Aleph' and 'Système' series – a departure from her usual more rounded shapes, initiated by a trip to Japan and the discovery of chaotic architectural ensembles. One of her proudest memories is of working at the illustrious Manufacture de Sèvres ('the porcelain was incredibly white, of the upmost quality'). 'The clay is everything to me,' she confirms. 'I like its simplicity. I'm fond of safe colours such as black, white and blue.' When asked what is the best compliment her work has ever received, Clémentine replies, 'There were no words, just tears of joy.'

See also pp. 259, 297
www.clementinedupre.com

1. Clémentine Dupré holding a 'Micro-organisme' bowl in Limoges porcelain with a translucent satin-finish enamel. The porcelain pearls were applied using a handmade rubber bulb fitted with a syringe.

2. A detail of 'Architecture Mobile #6' in porcelain chamotte and matt black enamel.

3. These 'Micro-organisme' vases are made of Limoges porcelain with a translucent satin-finish enamel on the inside and coloured porcelain pearls with a glossy translucent finish.

4. The apparently random nature of the 'Architecture Mobile #6' structure is intricately beautiful.

5. One of nine bowls from the 'Micro-organisme' series, all made of Limoges porcelain turned on a potter's wheel and all featuring hand-applied porcelain pearls.

6. Applying pearls onto a turned and sanded bowl, using a handmade rubber bulb that can be fitted with syringes of different diameter.

7. Memorabilia and items of research and inspiration surround small-scale structural templates – the basis for the 'Axiomatique' series – created during Clémentine's residency in Japan.

Content & Container

Germany

What if we had it all wrong, obsessing about perfection and being afraid to take risks? Pia Pasalk tirelessly designs functional objects that confront preconceptions, their revelatory messages delivering a jolt to the system. 'Appreciating the extra in the ordinary and understanding that perfection is an illusion are vital. If you start to pay attention, you will always find so-called blemishes. This is incredibly exciting, especially in our world, which is getting more and more superficial and absurd (e.g. Photoshopped reality),' asserts Pia. Her fixation on celebrating the 'imperfect' stems from her own personal struggles. 'I've been a stutterer since I was three years old. I therefore learned very early on that it's the supposed flaws that give life depth and make it multi-faceted,' she ventures. In addition, 'one of our three children has Down's Syndrome, so we are far from the social concept of the "perfect child", but she is amazing in her individual way. I think it's very healthy to get rid of the guidelines imposed by our performance- and consumption-driven society.' Pia realized that she revelled in exploring her own ideas and finding her style, after training as a goldsmith in Florence, so decided she would need to be her own boss. 'I studied product design at the Düsseldorf University of Applied Sciences

and the Birmingham Institute of Art and Design to get the best possible prerequisites for working independently,' she recalls. In 2008, she founded Content & Container in Cologne, producing high-quality collections by hand in small quantities. Benefiting from a multidisciplinary approach, each collection has its own socially charged manifesto: 'Parcelbag' tackles the fact that we often get more joy from anticipating the arrival of a parcel than in actually unwrapping it; 'Woodraw' emphasizes the sense of touch over sight; 'C-Set' consists of handmade utensils whose accidental defects take centre stage – a concept taken even further in the 'Perfect Imperfect' series. Pia exults in challenging notions of wrong versus right. 'When I presented my work for the first time at a trade show, some manufacturers were outraged that someone whose work mainly consists of the mistakes these same manufacturers seek to avoid in their own production processes could get given the "Young Talents" award,' she remembers with a smile. In 'revenge of the outcasts' style, one can now find her works in museums as well as design stores worldwide.

See also pp. 280, 303
www.contentandcontainer.com

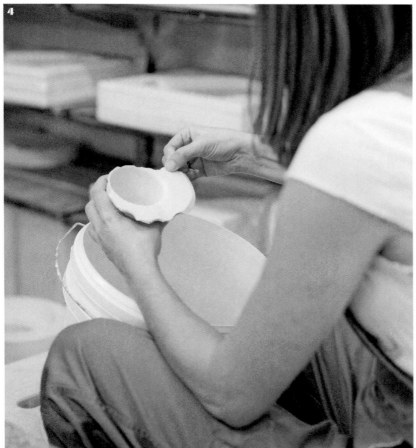

1. 'Perfection is an illusion,' says Content & Container founder Pia Pasalk. This slipcast porcelain plate and dish are from the 'Perfect Imperfect' collection.

2. Pia modelling her 'Perfect Imperfect' cup and saucer brooches in porcelain and sterling silver.

3. Each piece is unique: a display of plates, bowls, cups, saucers and vases from the 'Perfect Imperfect' collection.

4. Creating imperfection: a 'Red Flow' coffee cup from the 'C-Set' series in progress.

5

62

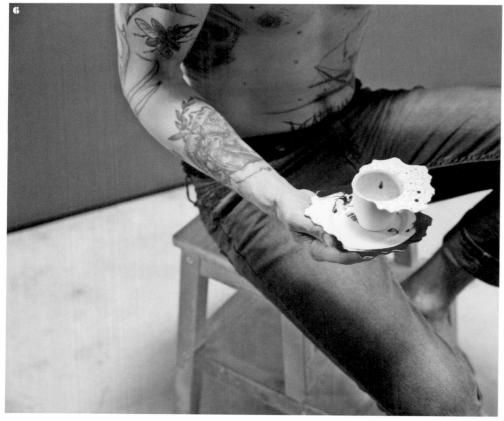

6

5. Casts and fired pieces are neatly stacked in Pia's studio.

6. A model holding a 'Blue Flow' saucer and 'Blue Dots' coffee cup from the 'C-Set' range.

7. The beauty within: 'Woodraw' vessels in different sizes, made of gold-plated slipcast porcelain.

7

Diana Fayt

USA

Combining loose geometry with artfully engraved organic figures, ceramicist-cum-storyteller Diana Fayt is inspired by a world of cartographical fantasy. The warped recollections of a 19th-century botanist, illustrated tales of ocean-going ships sailing in far-off waters, swallows gliding around dogwoods and poppies: these are the visions that nourish her artistic prowess. 'I've developed a technique that I refer to as "etching in clay", mimicking traditional drypoint processes used in printmaking but with a twist: I treat my ceramic surface as the etching plate. I carefully incise lines of different depths and widths, using an array of tools, to create movement. Each piece is individually hand-built or slip-cast.' Diana's original, free-hand drawings come complete with her signature markings: stippled dots, radiating shapes, random scratches and colour-block combinations. She tries to work as sustainably as possible. In some series, such as her scrimshaw-inspired works, she has addressed the issue of endangered species – her way of paying homage to nature and its inhabitants. Diana, who comes from a supportive family of artists, makers and circus performers, has been creating ceramics for nearly thirty years, starting out with traditional pots, then graduating to majolica glazes and hand-painted patterns. 'I've always been interested in surface treatments and my work has always involved drawing in some way, but my narrative has become more complex,' she observes. She had her epiphany at the age of 21, while visiting a friend's pottery class. 'I knew in that instant it was what I wanted to do, though I had no idea what that meant or how it would manifest itself,' she recalls. 'Now I love the visceral feeling of drawing into the clay surface and feel I've mastered the ability to create sensitive line quality in a material that isn't known to be sympathetic to delicacy.' Just touching Diana's plates and vessels is a spellbinding sensory experience. Indeed, she likes to discuss her work with a blind neighbour. 'I put it in her hands; let her feel it. We also discuss the way things "look" all the time. I describe the feeling of a colour or image, the narrative and process,' she recounts. 'It is beauty that we remember… not just physical beauty, but the beauty of kind words or a generous gesture. Thoughtfulness is also a beautiful thing. I like to make beautiful things that embody all of these qualities.'

See also p.298
www.dianafayt.com

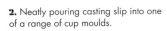

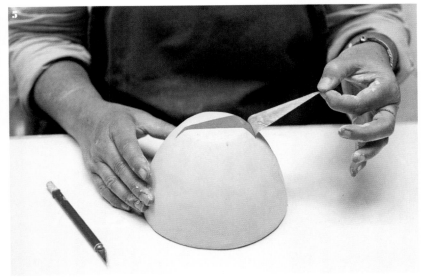

1. Diana Fayt selecting a form from a large assortment of handmade moulds.

2. Neatly pouring casting slip into one of a range of cup moulds.

3. Test tiles, which Diana uses to create her delicate colour combinations.

4. Every enchanting image is individually hand-etched.

5. Removing the stencil paper from a bowl to reveal a burst of colour underneath.

65

6. We would smile as widely as Diana if we were holding one of her scrimshaw-inspired platters.

7. We want them all! Shelves in Diana's studio filled with exquisite finished bowls, platters, plates and cups.

Domenica More Gordon

UK

Mementoes of loved ones are often cherished, but dog lovers in particular have long wished to commemorate their best friends. They can now enlist the services of Domenica More Gordon, an artist and writer who has been working with wool for some five years, handcrafting one-off animal figurines with extraordinary verisimilitude and a dose of levity. The detailing gives the impression the sculptures could actually be sentient. 'My aim in making a felt dog is to capture an echo of the attachment that I feel for my own dogs and that I used to feel for particular childhood toys,' says Domenica, noting that she finds herself particularly drawn to shy, noble and kind animals. 'I need to find that emotional connection.' She spent many years working for magazines, where, she says, 'I learned more about design and art than I did at art college'. Designing sets and photo shoots for *World of Interiors* and *Elle Decoration* taught her how to extract a story from an image, how to create atmosphere and drama from colour and texture, and above all, as she observes, 'to question myself and to ask why? Why do I like some things and not others? Why do some objects resonate and others leave me cold? My favourite things feel as if they have been made purely for the experience of making.' Her painter

father and sculptor/textile artist mother have also been a great influence. For her own art, Domenica starts with an image, idea or story that has moved her or made her smile, then she draws it and doodles around it. 'I always carry a sketchbook,' she enthuses, 'and draw or write down ideas. Sometimes I put things aside and pick them up later, when I can see with fresh eyes what needs to change to make it sing. It's this dance that intrigues me so much.' She also stockpiles newspaper cuttings as possible sources of inspiration. Her prowess in portraiture – which encompasses various animals, and includes the media of textile and illustration – has attracted a loyal following ('a high moment was when a gallery rang to say that Brad Pitt had just made an enquiry'). One customer was buried with her dog; another never travels without hers. Whenever Domenica holds an online sale, she puts all the bids into a hat and picks out names at random to give her many fans from different time zones a chance. She also works to commission, but the waiting list is currently over a year long. Surely the one drawback of being the Best in Show...

See also pp. 251, 279, 320
www.domenicamoregordon.com

1. Domenica More Gordon, perhaps contemplating one of her charming works.

2. Teensy-weensy handmade shoes, showcasing an extraordinary level of detail and designed for the 'Dressed Animals' range.

3. Archie, Domenica's dog and muse, is free to roam the studio, which is overflowing with materials, sources of inspiration and finished creations.

4. Domenica excels at narrating doggy adventures through her whimsical watercolour illustrations.

5. A gun dog inspired by a fuzzy photograph from a 1920s encyclopaedia of dogs.

6. Dressed to the nines: 'Donkey', one of many 'Dressed Animals' who all wear miniature renditions of clothes, bags and shoes by the Tokyo-based Arts & Science brand.

7. Domenica's dogs – unnamed unless made for specific commissions – are generally created around a particular collection, such as this adorable example from 'Show Dogs'.

Emmanuelle Dupont

France

It goes without saying that embroidery can turn any swatch of fabric into a beautiful textile…but it can also transform it into a spectacular work of art. Welcome to the chimerical wonderland of Emmanuelle Dupont, one of France's most gifted embroidery artists. Her mind is populated with strange forms, fantastical animals and exuberant plants. 'I see myself as a painter and sculptor, but foremost as an explorer,' she says. 'I freely compose and improvise depending on the materials and colours I come across, yet always with a poetic perspective. I dream my own microcosms. And what fascinates me about crafting by hand is the authenticity and uniqueness it offers.' Emmanuelle is a devotee of the countryside, where she lives and works, finding it an inexhaustible source of inspiration for shapes, colours and textures, such as butterfly wings, beetle heads and elytra, and the sloughed skins of snakes, which embellish her needlework with all their confrontational magic. 'My work invites the viewer to observe. Whether nature lovers or scared by wildlife, people never remain indifferent to my creations. It's fascinating, as I primarily create *trompe l'œil* and it feels as if people fall for it every time.' Emmanuelle established herself as a freelance textile designer and visual artist after

graduating with a degree in embroidery from the École Supérieure des Arts Appliqués Duperré. Collaborations with fashion and interior design companies were quick to follow: window displays for department stores; samples and patterns for haute couture; a project with a fine jeweler. Her creative mission includes exploring possible crossovers between different crafts, thereby applying embroidery to unconventional territories. Her proudest moment was creating the 'Phalaenopsis' work that won the Liliane Bettencourt 'Pour l'Intelligence de la Main' competition ('my aim was to create a masterpiece in which one would be unable to perceive the human touch; the illusion of reality, in essence'). Emmanuelle has also run workshops in India and Egypt, and teaches embroidery in France. 'As I keep learning new techniques, teaching helps broaden my skills and expands my sphere of activities.' She notes, 'I am very attuned to the plight of our planet and the human condition. One day, someone said to me, "Thank you for what you are offering us to see." I always hope people can sense that each piece is linked to my respect for Life.'

See also pp. 1, 252
www.emmanuelle-dupont.com

5

6

1. Emmanuelle Dupont adjusting a work-in-progress headpiece.

2. A detail of a 'Phalaenopsis Orchid': the silk muslin petals are satin-stitched and embroidered with black jet pearls.

3. The mesmerizing 'Phalaenopsis Orchids' duo, from the 'Chimères' series, look imperial thanks to their slightly menacing stature. Emmanuelle has applied numerous skilful techniques in their creation.

4. The 'Serpent Corset', an ode to Adam and Eve mythology, made of dyed shagreen patches sewn together, then demarcated with glass bead and Swarovski crystal embroidery. The head of the serpent is towards the bottom of the corset, with the wrought iron pole acting as its tongue.

5. Expert precision is needed to stitch each little bead around the snake-like shagreen scales.

6, 7. Stunning hues of silk threads and iridescent beads contribute to the precious aura of the 'Serpent Corset'.

Greg Hatton

Australia

'Bravo!' we should cry to anyone offering an alternative to our wasteful throwaway consumer culture. A welcome back-to-basics attitude is championed by furniture maker Greg Hatton, who had an epiphany while visiting a friend's great-uncle in remote Northwestern Victoria. 'Here was this old guy who had lived on the same property all his life, in very harsh farming land, but he had an inventive mind and through accident or purpose had created everything he needed out of stuff he had lying around: amazing resourcefulness and creativity.' Greg realized – after stints as a fisheries and wildlife officer, a bike courier, a vegetable farmer, a landscape gardener and a stonemason – that he had found his vocation. 'The passion for me comes from turning a raw material – the rawer the better – into something tangible, functional and hopefully beautiful.' He goes on, 'I often challenge myself to work loosely; to avoid making something as someone would expect. I remember making a coffee table for a photo shoot in about half an hour, with a pile of old casting timbers and a bradding gun. Nothing was square, but the accidental aesthetic was great.' Another key memory was of making his first chair for his mother from a tree that had fallen in the backyard ('a windfall, you may say'). Generally,

he starts with a design scratched out on a sheet of A3 paper with a blunt carpenter's pencil ('occasionally a client will want a drawing and then I have to smarten it up a bit'). His primary concerns are making pieces that last and ensuring a visual balance ('a table, for example, has to have a top in balance with the thickness of the leg'). Indulging his fondness for chainsaws, Greg predominantly uses timber, but he also strays into other areas such as stone and steel. 'I design from what I have, rather than seeking a material to suit a design.' Most of his timber is sourced from a local mill and he also utilizes 'environmental weeds' such as willows and poplars. 'I would like to see Australia value its resources a bit more, rather than chopping up our forests and sending them overseas as woodchips,' he notes. Meanwhile, he has been busy renovating his own home – 'a rambling multi-level old butter factory' – trying to 'add a bit of a contemporary touch without detracting from the old girl's beauty'. It's an approach that can be found in all of Greg's works: modern in their clever construction and intent, yet humble in their organic authenticity.

See also p.264
www.greghatton.com

7. A little helper lends a hand painting 'Beetlerack' stools.

8. Industrial meets organic in Greg's living room, where a 'Pipe Bender Experiment' lamp and a 'Beetlerack' stool become instant design statements.

79

6. The best of both worlds: silver birch legs and an antique table top comprise this gem of a dining table.

Hannah Waldron

UK

We picture explorers hopping on planes and reporting their experiences in leather-bound notebooks…but Hannah Waldron uses a portable loom and tells her stories through the art of weaving. 'I've travelled with my loom to various places,' she recounts. 'Weaving encourages in me a sensitivity to my surroundings. In one part of my "To Houshi Onsen" work, I've tried to describe visually the textures of the first Japanese meal I ate at the traditional *ryokan* where we were staying.' Expressing a keen interest in 'the mapping of experiences', Hannah explains, 'I draw upon a personal visual vocabulary of forms that aims to distil information to its most essential in order to make images that communicate broadly and might lead to personal interpretation.' She studied illustration at the University of Brighton, then later spent six months in Berlin, where she fell in love with the work of Anni Albers and Gunta Stölzl at the Bauhaus Archive. 'On my return to London, a friend was looking at my work and suggested that my mark-making, which used a grid structure with a lot of horizontal and vertical lines and hatching, would translate well into weaving. She gave me a quick lesson and I was hooked.' Passionate about learning new techniques on computer-assisted looms such as the 24-shaft Compu-Dobby

or the digital hand-jacquard, Hannah recently graduated with an MFA in textiles from Konstfack in Sweden. Graphic design continues to inform her aesthetic, with yellow and cadmium red as pictorial trademarks. 'Working as an assistant to the British artist Ben Johnson also gave me a real appreciation of methodology. His process is fascinating, with many stages from conception to realization.' Hannah now makes illustrations, tapestries and prints that have been reproduced on silk. 'I enjoy the constraints of working within a grid, but there's so much freedom for what can happen within that space. Tapestry is quite methodical and controlled but also rhythmic and full of joy.' Not long ago she was contacted by a woman who had seen her Edinburgh Art Festival map, which was partly inspired by Japanese Edo-period maps. The woman reported that she had instinctively begun to read the text from right to left: 'It made her aware of something deeply rooted in her, aesthetically. I was so glad the map had helped her find that connection.' Through Hannah's work, we can all appreciate the value of vibrant textile art.

See also p.305
www.hannahwaldron.co.uk

1. Elements of weaving: spools of yarn, grids and patterns.

2. Hannah Waldron passing the final shuttle to complete a piece. She weaves using her own unique tapestry style, which is based on a variety of techniques – ancient Peruvian and European, but mostly intuitively learned.

3. Hannah's work has been described as 'architecturally grounded in place but adrift in time'. This work in progress almost merges with her wall of inspirations.

4. A detail of a 'Venice Furoshiki' printed silk scarf attesting to Hannah's predilection for saturated colours, modernist patterns and cultural cross-pollination.

5. We would not mind getting lost in this stunning 'Maze Furoshiki' printed cotton scarf designed for Link.

6

6. Hannah adjusting her 'To Houshi Onsen' tapestry, from 'The Map Tapestries' series.

7. Hannah working on a portable loom which she has placed on a small bench in an exhibition space. She is raising the heddle to create the up-shed.

8. The 'Kreuzberg' design being woven on an Ashford rigid heddle loom. The cartoon and gouache paintings serve as colour and form guides.

7

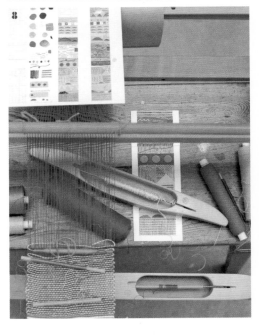

Hanne Enemark

UK

Diamonds are created under pressure: a concept that comes to mind when contemplating Hanne Enemark's stunning vessels. Firstly, like diamonds, glass requires high temperatures for energy-intense transformation; secondly, Hanne's glassworks use jewelry references – gold shimmers and gem-like ornaments – that exude understated luxury. 'Before I started working with glass, I dabbled a bit with making jewelry,' Hanne admits. She had never seen anybody blow glass before, but once she tried she was told she had a flair for it, 'so I just kept on doing it'. She studied glass at the Glass and Ceramic School on the island of Bornholm, Denmark, then did an MA at the Royal College of Art in London, and has now been working with glass for some thirteen years. 'My work has always had a very simple expression, but I think it's become more refined over the years,' she comments. Sophisticated hues such as ash grey, bronze and indigo blue are picked up by gold accents that artfully delineate an edge (the 'Cracked Rim' series), a section ('Choker' series) or a detail ('Cristal' series). Minimalist shapes are enhanced by organic adornments: quartz-cut, glass-blown crystals cling to the base of regal vases in the 'Cristallized' series, while gold-plated brass butterflies hover over the curvaceous surface

of lights for the 'Phototaxis' series and matching 'Imago' vase. To carry out the various techniques involved, Hanne spends a lot of time ferrying glass between studios: 'I normally blow my glass at London Glassblowing with my good friend and colleague Louis Thompson, and I also cold-work pieces there. For other elements, such as crystal shapes, I cast at Studio Manifold in East London, co-founded with close friends from the RCA. I also flame-polish and finish elements there, then return again to the blowing studio to attach the crystals. One of my colleagues says he has never seen me without a suitcase!' Hanne's ideas often arise during the process of making: 'noticing little things, refining these findings and translating them into a piece'. Innovative thinking is her mantra ('I recently used baking potatoes to make moulds that looked like quartz shapes'). Working with glass is a challenge, Hanne notes, 'but I always end up loving it. It's amazing to see the finished result, when you've been working on a piece for months and have resolved technical problems along the way and learned new things about the material and sometimes about yourself, too.'

See also pp. 2–3, 269, 285
www.hanneenemark.com

1. Hanne Enemark shaping a 'Fool's Gold' vase with a newspaper pad to achieve the desired curve.

2. A detail of a butterfly on an 'Imago' vase.

85

3. Hot glass sticks to hot glass: Hanne heating a rim in the reheating chamber.

4. A detail of an 'Imago' vase in blown and cast glass, its butterflies appearing to hover over the surface.

5. As precious as the gemstones by which it was inspired: a 'Cristallized' vase in blown and cast glass.

6

9. Intentional imperfection is the hallmark: vessels from the 'Cracked Rim' series, made of blown glass, platinum and 22ct gold.

7

8

6. The gold cubes of the 'Fool's Gold' vase (see also pp. 2–3) are made in several stages over several days. Here, Hanne is working with a cube on the rim of a blown piece.

7. Voluptuous and luxurious rolled into one: vessels from the 'Choker' series, made of blown glass, platinum and 22ct gold.

8. After glass has been gathered from the furnace, it is shaped with the use of a wooden block, then shaped again with a newspaper pad that has been soaked in water. Here, Hanne is using jacks to create a line, which will make it possible to transfer the shaped glass to a punty iron.

9

Iida-Kasaten

Japan

What could make you as happy for the rain to pour as for the sun to shine? The answer is a handmade, super-light, one-off umbrella by Yoshihisa Iida. 'Beauty is an essential part of my creations,' the craftsman remarks, 'because it's what makes life unique and colourful.' His custom-made accessories are on sale to the public through two annual exhibition events (parasols in spring, umbrellas in autumn). He also makes umbrellas for films and plays, and collaborates occasionally with other businesses. Every season he updates his collection of original textiles and adds approximately six new patterns. Orders are dispatched within three months. 'Some customers are shocked to learn they have to wait three months,' he comments, 'but I think it has gradually become a point of "uniqueness" for us. I also receive orders from retailers, but sometimes I have to reject these because the quantity I can make is limited.' Yoshihisa always has the end-user in mind. 'An umbrella is comprised of so many parts. Once I've designed the cloths, handles, buttons and metal fittings, I issue orders to the relevant factories and craftsmen. From the materials gathered, I then assemble and sew the product by hand. A fascinating aspect is that I can ponder, "What kind of umbrella do I want

to make?" while actually making the umbrella.' For his handles he often uses an unconventional ready-made component, such as an antique object found at a flea market, or an old insulator, or a spool of thread. For his parasol shades he generally uses cool linens; for his umbrellas polyesters. He majored in textile design at Tama Art University, learning traditional dyeing and weaving techniques as well as silkscreen printing, and decided to make his first umbrella to showcase one of his own textile designs. Key in his formation was umbrella craftswoman Tomoko Kamata. 'I heard that traditional umbrella craftsmen learn by watching their parents, so I watched Kamata.' Yoshihisa would then return home to modify his technique before bringing the results back to Kamata. 'I purchased an umbrella-making machine called "Pegasus", and Kamata offered me a rare antique wooden frame/mould that is indispensable,' he adds. His intention is to preserve and expand the development of Japan's umbrella tradition, and for his work to be displayed in galleries or museums, 'as my legacy'. Reason enough for us to sing in the rain...

See also p.278
www.iida-kasaten.jp

1. A colourful row of contemporary printed cotton parasols from the 'Ear Sticks' series.

2. Yoshihisa Iida at work, carrying out *tenjime* – a finishing step in the production process, referring to the tying of knots.

3. Yoshihisa cutting panels out of printed cloth.

4. The master and his team at work in the quintessentially Japanese workspace.

5. Summer calling! Delightful floral embroideries on cotton for parasols in the 'Sunflower' series.

6. Not just any sewing machine: the 'Pegasus' is a special resource for umbrella-makers.

7. A member of the team making 'wraps', which consists of preparing decorative parts for a parasol.

8. Bespoke umbrella and parasol handles, designed by Yoshihisa and produced locally in Japan.

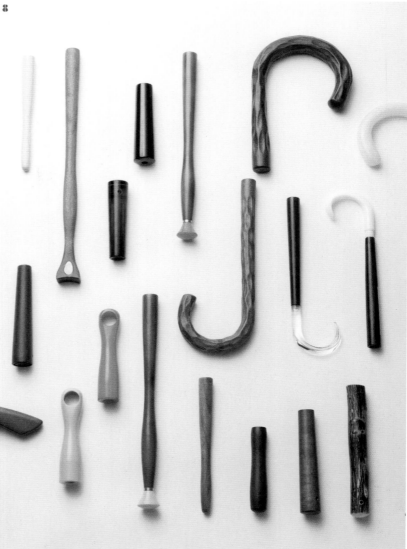

91

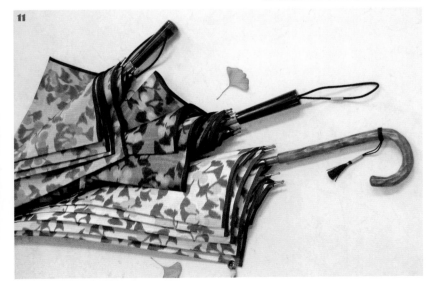

9. Unique details from top to bottom: here, examples of the carved wood 'Animal Handle' series.

10. The simple, peaceful, utterly artisanal studio.

11. Most of the prints that Yoshihisa designs are nature-inspired, including this elegant 'Gingko' series in *hogushi*-woven polyester.

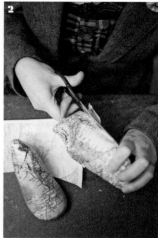

Jennifer Collier

UK

Hold onto your love letters. Jennifer Collier takes pleasure in turning sentimental correspondence into meaningful sculptures that emulate pleasing everyday objects. 'It's always quite scary cutting letters up,' she admits. 'I don't let myself read them, as I feel that would be an invasion of privacy and would make it even harder to use them.' For other elements of prized material – old books and photographs – she scours charity shops and flea markets. Most of her handmade creations are in simple cream, her signature colour by default. Sometimes the type of book informs the nature of the sculpture: pages from a gardening book, for example, might be used to create facsimile gardening tools. 'I never fail to get excited when I find a gem in a shop. My current favourites are cookery books that are splattered with food stains and have handwritten notes and measurements in the margin; second are children's books, where a child has loved the book enough to sit and colour in the illustrations,' she confides. 'When the narrative is obvious – for example, a camera made from vintage photographs – my time is spent devising a template. It can take many attempts to get complicated shapes and parts to fit together, so this phase is done in scrap paper. The final piece is made with found paper.

By having a template to draw around, I can remake each item to commission.' Jennifer's ultimate aim is to combine her passions for salvaged paper, literature and traditional embroidery techniques. 'I owe a lot to Amanda Clayton, the amazing tutor on my foundation course, who showed me there is more to art than drawing and painting, and introduced me to the world of stitch.' Jennifer went on to do a degree in textiles at Manchester Metropolitan University. Her favourite technique is 'Suffolk puffs' (or 'Yo-yos'), traditionally accomplished in fabric but here done with recycled scraps of paper. Everything happens in Jennifer's gallery and workshop space, Unit Twelve, created so that her admirers can see coherent collections of her work and so that she can share insights into studio life with her workshop participants. 'I always think seeing someone's studio is a bit like looking directly into their brain: neither should ever be too tidy,' she quips. Pondering her next challenge – constructing an entire room set, right down to paper tea set and armchair – she sums up, 'My works are nostalgic journeys with a twist of the unexpected.'

See also p.294
www.jennifercollier.co.uk

1. Say cheese! Jennifer Collier taking aim with her 'Map' SLR camera.

2. The whole world in her hands: constructing 'Map' baby shoes.

3. Knock, knock: the entrance to Jennifer's workshop is as delightful as her paper sculptures.

4. A trip down memory lane, one step at a time: stilettos, baby shoes and brogues made of an array of vintage books, maps and sheet music.

5. An example of poetic upcycling: 'Alice' kid gloves.

6. Every corner of Jennifer's workshop exudes old-world charm.

7. The 'Map' SLR camera, made of machine-stitched vintage maps and grey board.

8. Jennifer's personal Ali Baba's cave, with rows of old books, catalogues, works in progress and finished pieces occupying every nook and cranny.

Jeremy Maxwell Wintrebert

France

Hot liquid matter swirls sensually around the axis of a rod: this is creation occurring before one's very eyes. 'It is a passion that began the first time I saw molten glass,' says French/American glassblower Jeremy Maxwell Wintrebert. As with any birth, glassblowing comes with a certain violence – a respectful tug of war between creator and creation – but, once one starts, there is no option but to finish. 'I'm a very instinctive person. I go with my gut,' Jeremy observes. 'I'm an artist who expresses himself through a craft…which means I relate to both worlds and make them co-exist.' His childhood in Africa, followed by a move to France on being orphaned at the age of 14, have substantially marked him. 'When I started blowing glass, I made very figurative work that was inspired by my childhood. Since then it has become a lot more oriented towards design and abstract sculptural work.' On encountering glass, he decided to skip studying and to set to work right away. 'I only started developing my creative side once I became proficient with the processes. I do freehand blowing, which means I don't use any moulds. My main tools are heat, gravity and movement.' Jeremy takes pride in plying a trade that has become increasingly rare in the West. He adds, 'The long history of

secrecy with techniques and know-how have also created a dynamic that is closed and failing to find ways of adapting to current markets. But, although the challenges are huge and sacrifices many, it's what makes the process of existing as a glass artist so exciting.' Having fine-tuned his skills by glassblowing in many workshops, including in California, Florida, Washington and the Czech Republic, he holds a key memory of Murano in Italy – 'one of the meccas of my profession'. But this adept of *filigrane*, an old Venetian decorative technique, has nevertheless succeeded in moving with the times, and his own creative process is sure-footed. 'Fabrication starts with a pen and paper and goes through quite a bit of drawing. Then I have to organize the tools, colours and team. Once everything is aligned, the blowing starts. If I see the glass doing something unexpected, then I can easily follow it.' Key to everything is 'a great team'. This non-believer in hierarchy – especially the 'baseless hierarchy of Art at the top, Design in the middle and Craft at the bottom' – embraces his gift, creating objects that are the height of beauty.

See also p.286
www.jeremyglass.com

1. Jeremy Maxwell Wintrebert preparing glass canes to be brought up in temperature, then fused to the surface of a blown piece.

2, 5. 'Human Nature' installations: these blown glass cylinders are about exploring the creative relationship between humankind and nature.

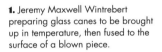

3. Torching a piece in between bouts of heating, which allows the piece to reach the precise level of heat desired.

4. Shaping with a wet newspaper while the vessel is being blown.

9. The 'Spirit Fruit' series in freehand-blown glass, using Venetian *filigrane* techniques, is about combining mastery of skills and the free-form beauty of hot molten glass – a combination that also symbolizes a feeling of release and change.

6. Blowing out the shoulders of a piece.

7. Reheating the glass to keep it soft and workable, and to prevent breakage.

8. A finished piece being detached from the pipe to be put in a cooling oven: it is still so hot that the assistant has to protect himself from head to toe.

Jevda

Sweden

Elaborate silks taken from antique Indian saris, embroidered fabrics from the Banjara tribes, suzanis from Uzbekistan, pompom decorations used for yurts and women's headdresses alike, traditional chapan overcoats, and little amulets from Pakistan and Afghanistan; not to mention pearls taken from French rosaries, precious lace sourced from an exclusive Belgian seller and mother-of-pearl buttons discovered in French flea markets. This could read as the bounty of some Silk Route odyssey, or a census of the best of traditional/old-world heritage…but, against all odds, these exquisite items are to be found in Gothenburg, Sweden. 'Textile artisan/couturier' Jenny Eve van den Arend, originally from France, is a free-spirited nomad who has found a sense of home in her collection of artefacts, which she masterfully assembles into sumptuous, one-off garments, following haute couture precepts. Stepping into her 'creative yurt', piled with remnants from across the world and across time, one almost feels as if one might encounter the Queen of Sheba herself. For each robe, colours and textures reflect abundance, but skilful layering conveys a sense of nobility. 'As soon as they don my creations, my clients exult that they feel like goddesses. They often say it's as if they're wearing a work of art. They say they can sense the love and patience I've dedicated,' Jenny Eve confides. She insists that she is simply a facilitator, giving random treasures the opportunity to come together. 'Inspiration always stems from the material. I never sketch, although I do project a 3D template in my mind.' She stitches her pieces by hand, constructing them on a seamstress's dummy while facing a mirror ('this allows the necessary perspective'). After many years using different materials, she notes, 'I am now confident enough to work with delicate vintage ethnic ornaments and cloths, which I call "beauties". In addition, I work with 19th-century laces and tulles, my first and enduring loves, still dyed with tea the old-fashioned way.' Jenny Eve's customers – true 'patrons of the arts' – embrace the fact that she offers the antithesis of seasonal fashion, in the form of a personal expression that celebrates both timelessness and made-to-measure exclusivity. 'As long as I can tell stories that enable people to escape their reality, and as long as I can inject some poetry into their lives,' Jenny Eve observes, 'it will feel as if I have accomplished my mission.'

See also p.276
www.jevda.blogspot.com

1. French-born Jenny Eve van den Arend resides in Sweden, but whenever strangers stop her, fascinated by her style, and ask, 'Where do you come from?', she replies, 'From my own world.'

2. Jenny Eve's self-confessed addictions: beautiful books and French rosary beads from the 1930s, '40s and '60s, which she uses in embroideries and on accessories.

101

3. 'L'Oiseau du Bonheur' (The Bird of Happiness) shawl, from the 'Nomades Célestes' collection: an antique sari that has been embroidered and ornamented.

4. Will it ward off negative spirits? A work-in-progress 'Vaudou' necklace featuring an African wooden mask, curtain tassels, *c.* 1930s/'40s French vintage boxwood beads and flat bronze beads from Ghana.

5. Fuchsia wonder: 'The Wild Berries' dress, a work in progress with embroidery in wool.

9. 'Sur un Air de Chagall': a vintage Uzbek woman's chapan in the process of being embellished and transformed.

6. 'Terra Nova' silhouettes, with neckpiece, stole, dress, cape and tunic: a textile symphony from India, Pakistan, Afghanistan, Uzbekistan and France.

7. Working on lavish neckpieces made of vintage fabrics from Uzbekistan and India, adorned with mother-of-pearl buttons and beads of glass and wood.

8. A cornucopia of exotic artefacts: *c.* 1920s purses from France and China, vintage ethnic necklaces, rare books, and silver champagne goblets containing pompoms and antique Afghan and Indian coins.

Jude Miller

New Zealand

Jude Miller's crepe-paper creations, with their exquisite level of detailing, are the ultimate in 3D trompe l'œil; so much so that occasionally butterflies have been seen hovering over freshly finished flowers. The tiny scale and the necessity for precision make the process extremely challenging and time-consuming. 'There's always some tricky corner I have to figure my way out of – sometimes by starting all over again – but I never give up,' Jude enthuses. 'The fact that my mind, eyes and hands work together like magic is captivating, and I've even become ambidextrous, which is handy!' The more Jude works with crepe paper, the more she understands what it can do. She also values highly the inspirational heritage of figures who have turned nature into art before her: the 18th-century embroideress and collagist Mrs Delany, the ingenious 19th-century glass-modelling Blaschka family and New Zealander botanical painter Fanny Osborne. It is easy to understand why Jude would love to be included in a botanical expedition, 'as the artist making models of rare flora in unexplored territory'. She first worked with paper in the early 1980s as an apprentice in a traditional *taller de cartonería*, or papier-mâché workshop, in Mexico. Six months later, she started to make paper hats, relishing the 3D surface. She eventually embarked on an art foundation course, followed by a part-time millinery course, but 'plants, flowers and trees have always been an essential part of my life, and in 2000 my need to do something new – and my having been given a huge stash of crepe paper – led me to start flower-making'. Originally a therapeutic hobby to give respite from a difficult job caring for elderly people, the craft soon turned into a passion. 'Bridal magazines started to contact me, but then I got sidetracked by weeds and humble roadside plants, and I began wandering the world to look at floral species in their natural places, which led me to horticultural societies.' This all came to a stop when, in 2008, Jude suffered major illness. She has only recently started working creatively again, and this time she is taking a delight in drawing nature with coloured pencils. Her small house in rural, coastal Aotearoa offers an environment full of inspiration. Jude says that all she needs is 'a flat surface and natural light', then she can produce what one of her friends has aptly described as 'absolutely original work with breathtaking details'.

See also p.293
www.judemiller.com

3. So visually intoxicating it does not need to be fragrant: puawhananga (*Clematis paniculata*).

4. True to its creator's heritage: a rata flower, fellow native of New Zealand.

1. Jude Miller can confirm that Mother Nature is a source of great joy!

2. A close-up of a strikingly life-like depiction of a pokeberry plant.

105

5. In Maori, 'kōwhai' means yellow, as seen in the kōwhai flowers of a local tree.

6. Nobody will mind if they can't get honey from this manuka branch.

106

7. Jude doesn't need many tools, just her years of experience and her prodigious gift.

8. One material stored in abundance: crepe paper in every hue.

9. Jude's work can also be viewed as a vital task: recording rare flora, such as the tawari tree native to New Zealand.

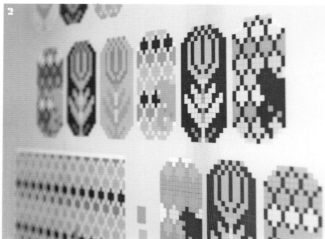

Karen Barbé

Chile

Meet a self-proclaimed 'craft guerrilla fighter', an expert who lives, breathes and dreams textiles. Chilean designer, embroideress, weaver and blogger Karen Barbé has devised the concept of the 'handmade lifestyle'. 'I value home, memories, cosiness and family, as opposed to fashion, appearance, future and over-exposure,' she declares. Four cornerstones anchor her work: a love of textiles (whether industrial, artisanal or artistic); an appreciation for humility ('an effort to portray the humble spirit, sense of aesthetics and colour of Chile'); nostalgia ('a trip to my own childhood and, by extension, an attempt to be a time-traveller through the review of old traditions and artifacts'); and the handmade ('a tribute to the time and love dedicated by all craftsmen to their creations'). A trained designer with a degree from Pontificia Universidad Católica de Chile, Karen won a scholarship to CSDMM/Universidad Politécnica de Madrid in Spain, where she gained a solid knowledge of textiles. After an unhappy stint in the corporate world, she was re-galvanized by a visit to Stockholm. 'Swedish design is inspired by tradition and craft, and that appeared to me to be a beautiful model to follow. I threw myself wholeheartedly into crafts as a reaction against the world of industrialization.'

The seeds had been sown years earlier, when the young Karen would sit by her mother's side and be encouraged to craft. 'I learned needlepoint embroidery on painted canvases using petit-point stitch,' she recalls. Since then, she has worked predominantly with natural fibres, such as cotton, linen, hemp and wool. 'I feel they add a certain nobility and finesse to my work, enhancing the painstaking handcraft. Besides, I feel I somehow become connected to the first primitive artisans who worked with materials sourced directly from nature.' Karen also favours neutral colours: ecru, beige, taupe, grey. 'They bring a soothing touch to my creations and help downplay tones that are too bright. On a more conceptual level, they make a connection with past times, before the arrival of synthetic fibres,' she observes. 'In addition, they are linked to the tones of worn textiles, thereby reinforcing my idea of nostalgia.' Karen shares her knowledge via embroidery workshops at her studio in Santiago, and this has invigorated her ambition to create a textile-related crafts school in Chile. This crusader wants to change our world one thread at a time.

See also p.310
www.karenbarbe.com

3. Karen working a needlepoint embroidery on a slate frame.

4. This embroidery detail appears on the back hem of a well-loved skirt.

5. Beautiful and useful: storage and a table-loom in the bright, neatly organized workshop.

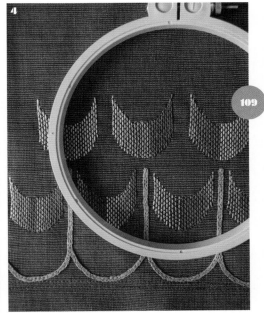

109

1. This detail of a photo tutorial – made for Karen Barbé's blog, and showing how to make woven patches for mending worn knits – is her most shared/pinned/'liked' image.

2. Karen plans and arranges the designs and colours for her embroideries on her computer.

8. Cooks, rejoice! An apron and a potholder worked in needlepoint stitch, in 100% wool with organic cotton sateen for backing.

110

6. A delightful screen-printed cotton twill tote from the 'Copihue' collection.

7. Keep nice and warm with this handwoven shawl/throw made on a rigid heddle loom with merino wool and angora hair.

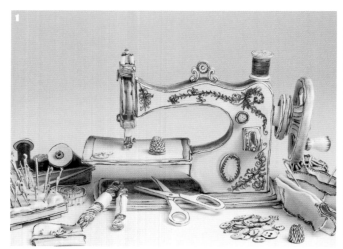

Katharine Morling

UK

Each of Katharine Morling's unique ceramic compositions looks like a pencil drawing come to life. This is partly because of their monochrome nature, but it is mostly because of the loose sense of movement infused into the solid structures: a *tour de force* that supports the optical illusion. It comes as no surprise that Katharine always kick-starts a project by producing a series of one-minute sketches. 'I try to get my unconscious ideas onto the page. I then look through my sketchbook and pick five or six ideas that appeal to me and work these up.' Now operating from Cockpit Arts in London, she has been working professionally with clay for some ten years. 'Originally my work was brightly coloured and glazed, inspired by my travels and nature, but when I found that I was feeling disconnected from it and it wasn't representing me anymore I spoke to Felicity Aylieff at the Royal College of Art and subsequently enrolled on an MA in ceramics and glass, where I developed my current unglazed style of black and white porcelain.' Katharine's repertoire encompasses still-life representations of familiar and functional objects as well as chimeras and hybrids drawn from her imagination. 'My pieces are truly personal creations,' she confirms. 'I create figurative and narrative works that contain emotions.' She adds, 'I'm happy when people can appreciate the dark, uncomfortable, uneasy side of my work, when they feel slightly on edge, as opposed to most people who see it as just quirky and fun.' She received early encouragement when a gallery bought ceramic work she had made when she was still at school, as well as pieces made at college. 'By the end of my degree, I thought I would try setting up a studio.' Katharine's enjoyment of her medium – working with porcelain straight from the bag, using her hands and a scalpel – resonates with her love of cooking. 'Handling clay has a peacefulness to it, and clay is a great medium for tapping into one's creativity. It also allows me to resort to three elements: vulnerability (if I wasn't showing my vulnerable side, I would feel I wasn't being truthful); endurance (the capacity to keep going, particularly in the early years when commissions are scarce); and joy (I love all aspects of the craft, from the making to the exhibiting and the great people I work with).' All these qualities are admirably on display in Katharine's artful tableaux.

See also p.257
www.katharinemorling.co.uk

1. A seamstress's fantasy, right down to the last fantastic detail: 'Stitched Up' in porcelain, with black stain.

2. Katharine Morling using a brush dipped in water to smooth the clay on her 'Kid Gloves' piece. She likes to paint onto a surface that has a smooth finish.

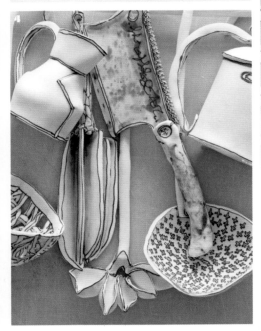

3. 'Armoured Eagle', a highly imaginative piece in earthstone and porcelain, with porcelain slip and black stain, from the 'Morling and the Hoard' series.

4. The tools of a charming trade: the 'Equipped' series of porcelain utensils.

5. Black and white has never been so delightful: Katharine uses her workshop to display her ceramic wonders and inspirational sketches.

D:69724

7. Bursting with still life: a 'Butterfly Garden' in porcelain and wire.

8. This jaunty cash register and accoutrements is made of earthstone and porcelain, and is fittingly titled 'Plenty'.

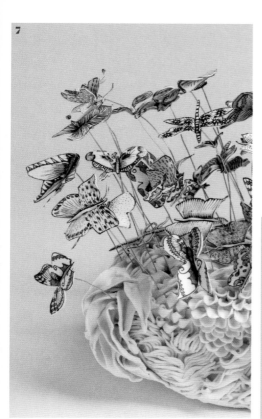

6. Porcelain components before they play their role in final compositions: each element looks as if it is worth collecting on its own.

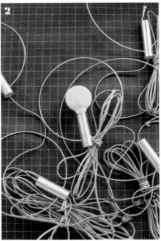

Ladies & Gentlemen Studio

USA

Ladies & Gentlemen Studio deserves thunderous applause for its well-designed domestic objects, which have the power to make one believe briefly that all is right with the world. The unambiguous simplicity is indicative of a razor-sharp eye and an uncompromising creative integrity. Dylan Davis and Jean Lee, the two design brains behind the Seattle-based brand, may be laying the foundation for a new sort of neo-classicism: part-Scandinavian in essence, part-Japanese in philosophy, always refreshing. Whether a mirror, wind chime or lounge chair, each piece offers something original and distinctive. 'An idea is usually born when a "need" meets a point of inspiration,' explains Dylan. 'That could be when a client asks us to design a light, or when we tell ourselves we want to create a serving tray. With a parameter in mind, we start exploring: looking through old books, browsing our collection of vintage objects, playing with material samples, or even going for a hike. After many different possibilities come about, one inevitably comes that is *it*. Another round of ideation then fills in the details, and we alternate between rough sketches, simple prototypes and basic CAD models to get there. Jean and I spend a lot of time going back and forth, coaching and critiquing

ourselves until the idea feels right. Our nature is to design products that are simple enough for us to make ourselves, and generally that's how the first ones are produced.' Ladies & Gentlemen Studio started as an online store for the pair's collected vintage artefacts. 'From this, we graduated to producing objects that repurposed or otherwise directly responded to a vintage object or idea. More recently we've focused on form and function – one step removed, but still related to vintage by material choices and mission.' The couple produce visually arresting compositions by playing with shapes, colours, objects and even negative space. While most of their materials aren't particularly unconventional, they assiduously strive to assemble them in unexpected ways. The challenges of being a small company with limited manufacturing capabilities have only bolstered their resourcefulness. 'We believe that if something is going to be made, it should be designed, produced and used deliberately and thoughtfully. We see our role as to create products that encourage people to engage with and respect what they buy.' Amen to that.

See also pp. 261, 282, 313
www.ladiesandgentlemenstudio.com

3

1. Dylan Davis and Jean Lee: a playful, über-creative duo.

2. 'Aura' lights in progress, available with brass or copper tubing.

3, 5. The whole is as beautiful as the sum of its parts: components for 'Aura' wind chimes.

4. A detail of an elegant 'Bell' chime.

6. The 'Aura' chimes series is a special-edition collaboration exploring sound and kinetics. Metal, wood and leather components by Ladies & Gentlemen Studio are combined with handmade ceramic pieces by Seattle artist Nicholas Nyland.

4

5

6

117

7. We have seen the light! Brass and copper ceiling lights from the 'Aura' collection.

8

9

8. The 'Ovis' lounge chair is Ladies & Gentlemen Studio's interpretation of a classic sling chair: a metal and whitened-maple frame supports a sling seat in leather or in natural wool hand-felted by textile artist Ashley Helvey.

9. Each 'Nyth' fruitbowl is constructed with liquid clay, layered in random splattered patterns until it is thick enough to form a mouldable slab that can be shaped into a bowl; the interiors are finished with clear glaze.

Leo Capote

Brazil

The workshop has all the hallmarks of a mechanic's den, laden as it is with pliers, pincers, saws and other tools...but the expected car or motorbike has been replaced with household objects and items of furniture. This is the cavernous studio of genius product designer and domestic-hybrid constructor, Leo Capote. He recycles his salvaged objects, depriving them of their primary purpose but grafting them together to make novel compounds that perform new functions, and appear to defy the laws of gravity while they're at it. 'I've been working on series of objects for nearly twenty years, constantly trying to figure out alternative ways of reusing things,' says Leo. 'Any industrialized objects with specific functions that have been designed using ergonomic, technological or formal principles, and that show particular finishes or manufacturing processes, are of interest for my practice.' The fact that the resulting specimens would not look out of place in a stylized version of *Transformers: The Movie*, minus the histrionics, speaks volumes about the majesty of their new-found character. Leo has been fixing and inventing things since he was a boy, and he vividly remembers being transfixed watching craftsmen at work. Having graduated in industrial design from the Universidade Paulista

in São Paulo, he has become a mainstay of Brazil's ever-growing design scene, and his works have also exported well, despite a very competitive international market. Part of his success can no doubt be attributed to his unusual creative process. He takes pleasure in the fact that nearly all of the components of his compositions, while appearing to be ordinary, in fact offer something special. Two types of functional creation are generally offered: 'the "free-flowing" one – no restrictions, pure free styling; and the one inscribed within a specific parameter or theme'. Leo can then deploy his uncanny ability to solder so skilfully that it is almost sensual, titillating our curiosity as we try to identify each object that has gone into a piece. 'I'm fascinated by the fact that one is able to execute an idea shaped in one's mind without needing a fully laid-out plan,' he remarks. 'The aim is to assemble freely, thus bringing surprise. I also try to avoid using too many colours, as I want to bring attention foremost to the object as a whole.' The Dada-esque quality of Leo's assemblages is sure to captivate onlookers for generations to come.

See also pp. 267, 283
www.leocapote.com

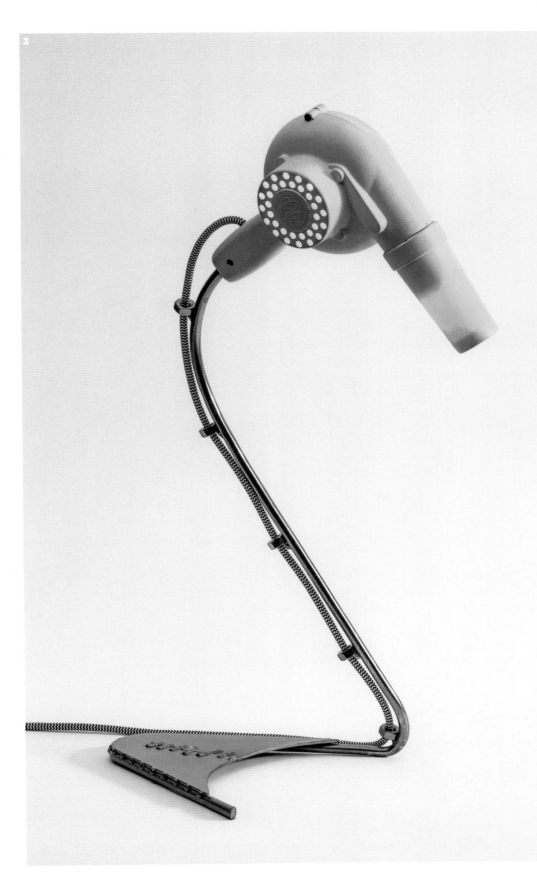

1. Leo Capote is a master at re-purposing bits of equipment into fun, utilitarian pieces.

2. A jigsaw of sharp tools forms a fragile equilibrium: the 'Luminária Bololo Sargento' lamp.

3. It's not what it seems: the humorous 'Luminária Secador de Cabelo Amarelo' lamp consists of a 50-year-old Swiss hairdryer on a base of steel with an oxidized nickel finish.

4. Leo's workshop is a cross between a mechanic's garage and an industrial laboratory.

5. How the mundane can morph into the exceptional: the 'Poltrona Pregos' armchair is made of 3,800 nails welded together and finished in electrostatic coating.

6. If you put together a fan of trowels, some spanners, a jigsaw of monkey wrenches, and some pipes and lug wrenches, what would you make? Leo made the 'Bololo Pedreiro' chair.

7. The 'Cadeira Panton Porcas' (or Panton Chair with Nuts) is an homage to the classic Verner Panton design, recreating its signature ergonomics through the assemblage of 680 steel welding nuts with red powder coating.

7

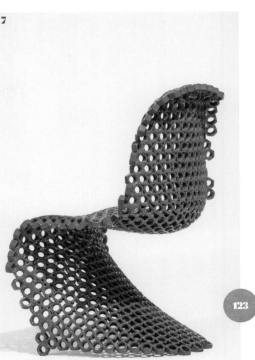

123

6

Lise Meunier

France

It is easy to fall for the delicate compositions made by Lise Meunier. This poetic artist meticulously constructs tableaux that evoke folk and religious art, using components such as ceramic flowers and coral, antique fabrics, vintage lace, golden leaves and found trinkets. 'I'm fascinated by the story that each piece conjures up through its errors and imperfections; anything that makes it a one-and-only and conveys the imprint of its maker,' Lise observes. Most of the time she begins by making random clay elements, with no precise idea of how they will ultimately be incorporated. 'Once they're baked and enamelled, I start to build little *bas-relief* still lifes, while adding components found in antique shops, on the street or in nature: I use a lot of textile and botanical remnants. Lastly, each creation is sealed under convex- or dome-shaped glass, which gives it a sort of imaginary preciosity and reinforces the idea of fragility.' The initial work with ceramics is multifold and time-consuming. 'Clay needs to be worked for a long time to soften it and to expel eventual air bubbles that could ruin the baking. I extract small pieces directly from plaques of clay that I've previously cut to measure. Later I slipcast the pieces together, then engrave the details. I let them dry, then sand them down before a first baking at 1000° in

the kiln, which gives a biscuit. I coat this with a clear enamel, the *couverte*, which will provide the sheen after a second baking at high temperature.' Lise notes that, while she may not continue to use clay in the long term, textiles will always remain part of her creative signature. 'My grandmother used to create costumes for shows, and I spent many childhood years surrounded by cloth and sewing machines.' Despite this promising start, actually becoming an artist seemed an inconceivable goal. 'I dared not even mention the idea, so studied art history as a compromise. I then became an agent for illustrators, and later a stylist and designer for lifestyle magazines and publishers, while always creating for myself on the side.' Having finally achieved her dream, Lise is mindful of her working practices. 'I need to work on my own, knowing there are no time constraints. This allows me to inhabit my own Self. Most important is access to natural light. I cannot stand it when the days shorten!' We, on the other hand, can always immerse ourselves in her enchanted works, the sealed *natures mortes* like promised lands steeped in simple beauty.

See also p.254
www.lise-meunier.blogspot.com

1. Lise Meunier, framed by her ravishing works.

2. Botany meets poetry: a still life of enamelled faïence flowers, textiles and plants under glass.

3. Will these ex-votos give us a wave? Arm charms made of enamelled faïence, with feathers and antique cloth.

4. Some of the pretty trinkets that Lise collects for future use.

125

5

lise meunier

6

7. Making exploratory marks in rolled-out clay.

8. In the manner of the Dutch masters: 'Nature Morte Fleurs à l'Oiseau Jaune' (Still Life with Flowers and a Yellow Bird).

9. A profusion of floral porcelain.

127

5. Something to add glamour to any cabinet of curiosities: a display of enamelled faïence flowers, a crochet textile and real plants.

6. Blooms captured for eternity: flowers in enamelled faïence with lace and antique textiles, preserved under glass domes.

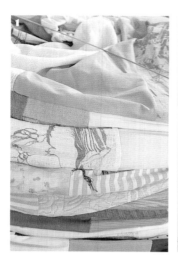

Maartje van den Noort

Netherlands

You might think the cataloguing on paper of avian species such as *Sturnus vulgaris*, *Passer domesticus*, *Pica pica* or *Corvus monedula* is the work of a scientist. But the realization that the birds may come embellished with collars of floral patterning gives away the fact that we are in the presence of an artist more than an ornithologist. 'I love to draw simple, comforting things like birds and plants,' says Maartje van den Noort. 'Every season, every year, they come back according to their own unstoppable cycle. Finding "Home" is a big underlying theme in my life and work.' Buildings are also subjects of interest. 'They make me wonder, "Who's in there? Do they feel at home?"... "Do I feel at home where I am?"' An illustrator with an eye for atmospheric muted scenes, Maartje works from a studio in central Amsterdam, between the National Maritime Museum and the Hortus Botanicus botanical garden. Pens are her tools of choice (she currently favours very fine German liners). She also uses etching and other traditional printing techniques to help her achieve the demarcations she relishes: 'rough yet fragile black lines, both steady and uncertain at the same time; and I love to use greyish colours, together with all sorts of whites for the background'. Maartje sometimes fixes

things during the drawing phase, but she never erases anything: 'This forces me to deal with what I have.' Challenging moments include knowing how to start, when faced with difficult techniques and heavy machinery, and knowing when to stop. By her own admission, Maartje works best when she has a specific assignment, image or deadline, but sometimes it is enough for her to look at an old photo to kick-start a project that will ultimately take on a life of its own. 'Every print has its own "ink character". When it's winter and I have cold hands, the ink won't run as smoothly as on a summer's day. I really appreciate the coincidental aspects of each work, and the fact that it doesn't have to be perfect.' Her artworks can be used in versatile ways, such as being applied to cushions, scarves, lightshades and stationery – perfect accessories for the boho-chic lifestyle. Maartje's love of flora and fauna, and her compassionate nature, shine through. Indeed, she confides that she could have worked in the social sector or in the field of creative therapy. Some of us might say that her drawn scenography provides us with exactly what we need.

See also p.314
http://maartjevandennoort.nl

1. A stack of collected fabric swatches with silkscreen-printed pieces, awaiting use as 'Lampions' (see **9**).

2. In the studio, a few simple brushstrokes reveal a compelling black bird.

3. Maartje van den Noort's wall of inspiration is a work of art in itself.

4. These 'Birds' postcards attest to Maartje's exquisite style of illustration.

5

130

5. Inking the printing plate with thick etching ink.

6. The print is revealed after being passed under the etching press's heavy metal roller, which transfers ink onto the damp paper.

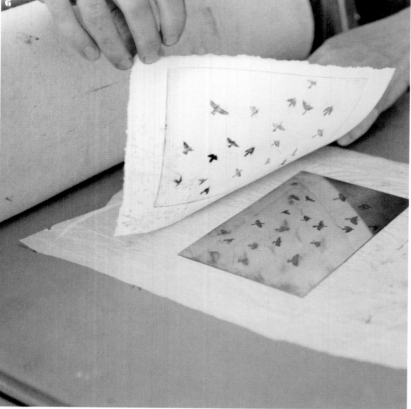

6

7. Maartje's studio is located in a converted 18th-century sailor's home: she shares this with three other artists, each having their own space.

8. A patchworked scarf mixing silkscreen-printed and plain fabrics.

9. 'Lampions' in full bloom.

MILOU

Maïssa Toulet

France

'I have resolved the conundrum about what is beautiful versus what is ugly. I simply decree beautiful anything that touches me,' declares French artist Maïssa Toulet. Through her work – a cross between white witchcraft, Assemblage Art and modern cabinets of curiosity – she metaphorically soothes her troubles by harnessing her beliefs and desires and laying bare her dreams, regrets and vulnerabilities. What she creates unearths who she is, like a symbolic and impenetrable language for private use only. 'I can scan any second-hand shop or rubbish bin and zoom in on exactly what I'm after. I forage broadly, ultimately marrying organic matter to manufactured components. This means combining plastics and chemicals with birds' wings, resin teeth, human hair, dried spiders, fish bones, bramble thorns, urchin spikes and boars' feet.' The outcome is often described as 'creepy', but this misses the point: Maïssa pairs the natural with the synthetic 'in order to inject slices of life into each artwork'. She obsessively recycles so that she can preserve things. 'It's my way of craving the eternal ever-after,' she reasons. 'My works are like rituals.' This accidental artist compensates for her lack of formal training by using her imagination and resourcefulness to the full. 'I experiment constantly,

and I learn from my mistakes. Discovering new tools, such as the Dremel drill and UV glue lamps, and new materials and knick-knacks such as miniature porcelain dolls, plastic toys and insects, enthrals me. But I can be very impatient and skip fundamental steps, which is absolutely contrary to being a good "maker". Let's say I am a hopelessly disorganized dreamer,' laughs Maïssa. Having said that, each composition is the result of methodical procedures: gluing tiny seeds one by one, or drilling precise holes through a mould to transplant small plants. 'In my topsy-turvy workshop, I simultaneously hold several stations of what I call "transformation": images are cut, scanned, resized and fitted on medallion cards, while found objects are moulded, painted, burnished and see-sawed; insect and egg shells are emptied, glass discs are pierced, cloths are dyed, leaves are stuck onto pint-sized trees and metal wires are bent into shape. The last phase – when I gather all the modified elements and assemble them into installations – is probably my favourite.' We are left with an exalted fantasy narrative: a work of art to decipher for a lifetime.

See also p.248
www.maissatoulet.fr

1. Maïssa Toulet meticulously painting a cut strip of paper.

2, 4. 'Adam et Eve' and 'Le Mariage Fâcheux' are part of the 'Arbres Généalogiques, Secrets de Famille' series. The collages are made using recycled plants from the Museum of Natural History in Paris, photo-story romance images from the 1950s and '60s, and texts cut from old books.

3. A satirical reinterpretation of a 19th-century wedding cake, 'Moutarde de Ménage' is part of the 'Marches Nuptiales' series. The cake toppers are antique, and the images and texts have been cut from old almanacs.

5

6

5. Body parts galore: small casts that have just been painted.

6. Death: one of Maïssa's favourite subjects. She plays down its morbid aspects by raising the aesthetic stakes, as in 'Série Vanités 1'.

7. This work was inspired by a Francis Ponge poem, 'Notes pour un Coquillage', a meditation on the human condition faced with natural cycles and time passing. Human figures are covered with algae and sea parasites, like wreckage on the ocean floor.

Manuela Castro Martins

Portugal

A resolute left-hander, Manuela Castro Martins used to be renowned for her clumsiness. Extraordinary, then, that some twelve years ago she abandoned a successful career as a community lawyer to devote herself to the art of glass-making. The transition was not quite as dramatic as it sounds: 'As a lawyer, I supported a community that lived on the very edge of survival; people living in places of extreme ugliness and yet capable of creating the most pure beauty. The experience made me very aware that beauty can turn up in the most improbable of locations.' Passionate about all spheres of human activity, Manuela embraces all forms of art. 'Literature is a strong source of inspiration, as seen in some of my works, such as "Other Portuguese Letters" inspired by a 17th-century book, or "Waiting for Odysseus", in which objects transform themselves into embroidery made of glass, reflecting on a question arising from Homer's *Odyssey*.' Poetry has also been a constant companion in the search for beauty, from José Régio's 'Cântico Negro' to the work of Natália Correia. 'This is the challenge I face every day: will I be able to create some beauty?' muses Manuela. Her process always starts with careful planning. 'When I finally decide to make the piece, everything then seems a lot simpler. It begins with cutting glass sheets, then setting the pieces to the intended design and finally flat-fusing them in hot kilns. The kiln stage lasts for at least 24 hours, but a longer fusion cycle may be needed depending on the size and thickness of the piece. Meanwhile I prepare moulds. Shaping only happens after fusion, by placing the piece over the mould, then returning it to the kiln.' Some pieces, including Manuela's colourful, textural 'glass lace' work, which has been awarded the Emerge design prize, can take over a week to make. She also produces utilitarian objects that are as 'clean' as possible. No matter what the project, she revels in the peace and quiet of her rural home and adjacent workshop. 'The sound of silence in this stunning countryside inspires my working days. Above all, I must be alone.' Manuela can then apply the two cornerstones of her work ethic: persistence ('you spend time feeling discouraged and then you have moments of pure ecstasy with the smallest, most unexpected solution') and discipline ('the ability to strip your life of the superfluous, so that you can dedicate yourself to the essential').

See also p.268
www.manuelacastromartins.com

3

4

5

6

7

8

1. Multicoloured sheets of glass are filed away in wooden crates.

2. With geometric precision, Manuela Castro Martins cuts glass sheets into rectangles, squares and other shapes before assembling her pieces by colour and material.

3. Weaving with glass: 'Glass Lace II' in blue.

4. 'Glass Lace I' in green and silver.

5. Highly tactile and most intriguing: the 'Impossible Jar I' in red glass, from the 'Waiting for Odysseus' collection.

6. Manuela's pieces are fused in kilns that can reach temperatures of 800°C.

7. An eerie presence: rows of ghostly moulds awaiting their purpose.

8. Cut pieces assembled on a mould to give the finished object the desired shape.

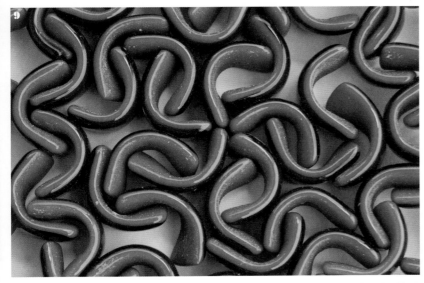

9. This detail from 'Glass Lace II' is a symphony of red and grey.

10. Red-hot: 'Glass Lace I' in red and silver.

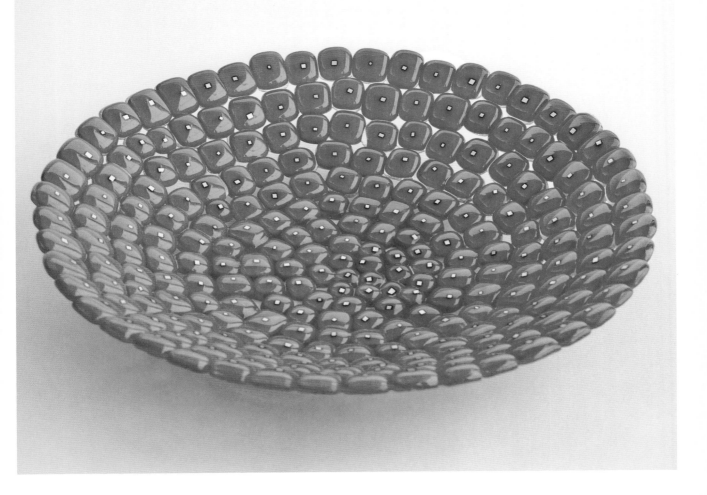

Margit Seland

Netherlands

Scandinavian design is famous for its ingenious minimalism – stylishness devoid of extravagance – and, luckily for us, this sensibility can be exported. Margit Seland first trained as an art teacher in her native Norway, specializing in textiles, but her studies included an exchange year in the Netherlands. She eventually completed a degree, in 2000, at the Department of Ceramics at the Gerrit Rietveld Academy in Amsterdam. Margit's approach to ceramics may well have been influenced by her longstanding enjoyment of working with various materials and techniques. 'Multitasking is an integral part of my life, as much as flexibility and a multimedia approach,' she confirms. 'As far back as I can remember, my three sisters and I were always competing for the sewing machine to develop our creative designs! Later, both as a teacher and as a sales assistant in an art gallery, I was really inspired by interactions with people. Meeting and communicating in different languages constantly inspires me in terms of seeing and dreaming about forms, colours and techniques.' In all Margit's work, one can also trace strong links to nature, the circle of life and the ecological footprints we leave behind. 'I want the people who purchase my work to feel that the piece of art they buy from me will enrich them;

that it will bring something new to their experience of enjoying a simple cup of tea or appreciating the beauty of flowers,' she muses. Her collections range from the poetic (smooth, pebble-shaped weights that are reminiscent of shells; ceramic pods on ribbon that are vases turned into wearable necklaces; vessels of different heights in a soothing palette of pastel stripes) to the more out of the box (a ceramic dish whose handles are made out of colourful rubber tubes affixed with the type of screw frequently used by plumbers). 'My style is in a way both simple and exclusive; both basic and complex,' says Margit. 'For me, a good creation is a combination of a unique, original idea and solid, proper craftsmanship. I thrive on the belief that one day most people will cherish the things that last: less mass-consumption and more uniqueness.' Margit's to-do list includes teaming up with professionals in different fields to develop meaningful new projects. 'To make something collaboratively with other artists/ designers would enrich so many people – even working as a generator for others' creativity – thus reaching far beyond myself.'

See also pp. 278, 299
www.margitseland.com

TRICOTECH (R) dlc DOUBLE LAYER CONSTRUCT

143

7. The variety of Margit's productions requires space, tables at different heights and, above all, a steady stream of daylight.

8. Springtime! 'Tide' jugs and cups in cast, coloured porcelain, with various oxides, glazes and sulphates.

9. Wait in line and everyone will be served: liquid clay, plus moulds.

1. Muted, refined colours for the 'Pinched Pitcher' jugs and cups in cast porcelain.

2. Margit Seland happily smoothing 'Pebble' bowls and cups with a sponge and water.

3. Fruit is instantly enhanced against the subtlety of these 'Pebble' side dishes and plates in cast porcelain.

4. Thinking outside the box: a zingy 'Wire' container in hand-built stoneware and porcelain, with rubber tubes and metal.

5. 'Phases' vases in coloured cast porcelain, with various glazes and ribbons, to embellish either your walls or yourself.

6. Breaking the mould.

Matthias Kaiser

Austria

The main room contains an adobe floor, windows facing a brook and a cherry tree, two Japanese-style kick-wheels with wooden wheel-heads, a large maple table and antique furniture from India. This is not a dealer's showroom or an Oriental workshop, however: it is the studio of the well-travelled ceramicist Matthias Kaiser, located in his 900-year-old home in the Austrian province of Styria. 'I studied product design with a focus on ceramics at Parsons School of Design in New York and at the University of Applied Arts in Vienna; I also did two apprenticeships with potters in Seto and Karatsu in Japan. Not directly related to the craft, I studied Sufi mysticism for more than a decade with a dervish in Tehran.' Working with clay has enabled Matthias to combine his interests in artistic expression with his love of nature (both parents are biologists) and also to enjoy the balance of physical and intellectual input that is required. 'First, I give a lump of soft clay a hollow shape and thus define the inside and part of the outside,' he explains, 'then, after the clay has hardened for a day or two, I trim it. I approach this give-and-take as an artistic endeavour within a tight framework of static and functional concerns, which makes it even more challenging.' Going to considerable lengths to improve his already vast

knowledge, Matthias excels at getting proportions right and refining subtle interventions to achieve meaningful yet understated outcomes. His perfectly executed minimalist forms are peppered with idiosyncrasies, namely irregularities in the ceramic bodies and glazes. 'Even though most of my work is functional, I don't look at it primarily from that viewpoint. I work on the shape and surface as on a sculpture,' says Matthias. 'I aim to create comprehensive simplicity. The best compliment I could receive is if someone tells me they use a piece every day.' While he takes delight in exploring the different components of clay, such as alumina, silica and iron, which he has fired in unusual ways, he is also open to working with any material that might suit a project – welded steel, plastic, wood and taxidermy so far among them. Collaborating with other artists, including Uchida Kouichi in Japan, is also a major foundation of Matthias's philosophy. 'I see my work as a delicate form of communication between people I may already know, people I may never have met in person, or people who may not even have been born yet.'

See also pp. 258, 301
www.matthiaskaiser.com

1. 'Facet' vases with a variety of iron-, cobalt- and copper-coloured glazes, which have a tendency to run as they melt during the firing phase.

2. Matthias Kaiser turning a ceramic piece in a pared-down setting imbued with aesthetic asceticism.

3. The stoneware 'Wayward Madara' vase ('madara' being a wheat straw ash glaze) has a delightful, eccentrically positioned neck.

4. The master at work on the potter's wheel.

5. A stoneware 'Jar with Snailshell Glaze'.

6. The stoneware 'Cracked Slip' sake server, evoking archaeological finds.

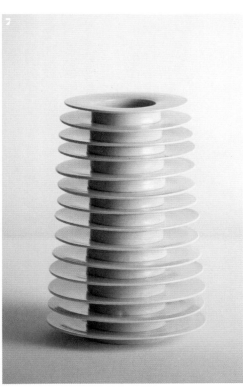

7. A deliberate 'accident' in the kiln: for the 'Stack' vase, fourteen porcelain bowls have been stack-fired together.

8. This porcelain vase on a sand base has been gradually built up with coils and paddles to give it a hexagonal shape.

9. This stoneware *chawan* (or tea bowl), made with a glaze containing wheat straw ash, feldspar and wood ash, also has a patch of iron ore glaze on one side. The combination is inspired by the traditional Karatsu style of Japanese ceramics.

10. A 'Copper' vase in stoneware.

147

Maxime Leroy

France

The fine art of *plumasserie* (the handling of feathers) is nowadays the work of a modest guild, mastered by a few independent artisans and mostly used in haute couture; it has nothing to do with commercially driven examples of careless application of cheap feathers as a trendy add-on. Here, plumes are considered exquisite ephemera. While their precious fragility is a drawback for most — no machine can process them and they degrade with time, like all matter — for *plumassiers* they are gold. Buoyed up by this exclusivity, the self-styled 'musician of feathers' Maxime Leroy has taken it upon himself to put feathered creations on an accessible pedestal. He likes to use plumes in unconventional circumstances, yet for everyday use. 'Sometimes I feel like the ugly duckling of the feather world, as my creativity runs wild. My only limit is in respecting the material,' he says. 'I aim to create feather ornaments that seep into normal life; a way to reconcile the democratization of the art of feathers on the one hand with the retention of their noble, unique quality on the other.' Aside from the day-to-day operations that come with managing orders — including preparing, calibrating and steaming feathers — Maxime constantly searches for original ideas and solutions. While all of his stock is sourced

from farmed birds, he occasionally unearths rare feathers from endangered species by rummaging through old stock and private collections. He has carved a small workshop space out of his apartment, but the boundaries are fluid as Maxime has surrounded himself everywhere with objects that fuel his inspiration — animal skins, stuffed birds, reptiles and insects — and has used cement and leather as the two main decorative accents. He first stumbled upon *plumasserie* as a form of artistic expression after being forced to give up a career as a contemporary dancer. 'I met Dominique Pillard during an open-house event at my college. He was there to introduce *plumasserie*, along with other participants presenting their trades. I found in feathers a similar ability to dance, bend and move that immediately appealed to my sensibility.' A famous designer once told Maxime that he offers 'a graphic re-interpretation of feathers that is novel'. Maxime keeps his imagination racing by collaborating with fellow designer trailblazers, showing through lyrical visions how feathers can enhance an ensemble while also being an integral part of it.

See also p.280
www.m-marceau.com

1. In this case, the dog owner does not look like his pet: Maxime Leroy and his devoted bulldog, Macho.

2. Securing individual feathers to the grid of a headpiece.

3–5. The feathers have been cut into arrow shapes to give the headpiece its 'forward-pointed' style, like a revisited Louise Brooks-type bob.

6. The flames spilled by the 'Paradis Dragon' brooch are made of bird of paradise and tragopan comb feathers.

7. 'Tragopan' earrings display delicate feathers from the body of the tragopan pheasant.

8. Stylish footwear to be snapped up by the god Hermes, or any self-respecting hipster: 'Sacco Baret No. 1 – Grey Sneakers' featuring turkey coquille (breast) feathers.

9. 'Sacco Baret No. 2 – Python Black Sneakers' pair streetwear cool with luxury.

Michaël Cailloux

France

Looking at a painting or even a frame, the emphasis is never on the wall behind them. So, when an artisan comes along with an idea to create 'jewelry for walls', one is wise to pay attention. Each of Michaël Cailloux's one-off, old-world creations stems from a marriage between two techniques, jewelry-making and etching. Michaël intends each piece to evoke the *mouche*, or 'beauty spot' fashion of the 18th century, a copper artwork beautifying a wall in the same way as aristocrats beautified their powdered faces with a painted mole. 'For twelve years I worked with two colleagues, mainly on ceramics and serigraphy, under our LZC brand, then I visited the permanent exhibition of jewelry at the Art Deco museum in Paris and was transfixed,' recalls Michaël. 'The next day, while etching at a class I had signed up for, I thought, "What about mixing the two?" I took my saw and a plaque of zinc, and I carved something – ultimately my first ever piece, the "Ombrelle" comb. Lacking experience, I let it sit in the acid bath for too long… Nevertheless I carried on and it all fell into place. Later I switched to copper for better results.' It took about four years and a lot of experimentation for Michaël to devise techniques that allowed him to design thicker lines, and his process is still a

work in progress. Each piece takes about a year from initial idea – which he arrives at after an intensive research phase, 'notably at the Forney library, which I love' – to hand or computer drawing. 'I apply the drawn composition to a copper plaque and cut it out with a bocfil saw. I engrave the plaque, then print a limited edition to obtain my "mouches estampillées" engravings. Finally, I shape and give volume to the plaque with a rivet setter and a chisel to create the wall jewelry that I call "mouches".' Accidental mistakes are only catalysts for further work. Each "mouche" (the word also means 'fly' and accounts for the signature emblem that is incorporated into every creation and 'disturbs the gaze', as Michaël quips) contains nods to 16th-century still lifes, imbued with references to flora and fauna. Michaël also designs collections of wallpaper and scarves using his initial sketches. Fittingly, he has been art and education director of the École Supérieure d'Art Françoise Conte since 2009. His ebullient curiosity and passion for the arts are sure indicators that he will be continuing his unusual botanical explorations.

See also pp. 253, 280, 292
www.michaelcailloux.com

1. Where it all begins: Michaël Cailloux making a drawing.

2. Unparalleled manoeuvrability thanks to the bocfil saw, which is used to cut out the intricate patterns of the drawing template placed on the copper plate.

3. Inking the copper design.

4. A bucolic trompe l'œil: 'Fable 02', an etched copper wall decoration, from the 'Grigris' series.

5. 'Aquarium', an etched copper wall decoration from the 'Natures Mortes' series.

6. Engraving is the crucial step to add the fine details.

7. Gently shaping the copper design with a bouterolle.

154

8. Bountiful flora and fauna: an Art Nouveau-inspired print for the 'Jardin d'Hivers' (Winter Garden) silk scarf.

Miga de Pan

Argentina

'Who's going to buy your dolls? Your friends? I thought this was just a hobby,' exclaimed Adriana Torres's boyfriend when she told him that she was going to do embroidery full-time. But, unbeknownst to her immediate circle, Adriana, aka Miga de Pan, had been quietly working on her stitching skills and forging a unique and highly desirable style. She had learned how to embroider while still working as an art director and graphic designer. 'I quickly realized that I was the only illustrator-embroiderer in Buenos Aires, so I sent my portfolio to what I thought was the "cutest" gallery in the city at that time. To my delight, they invited me to take part in their shows.' This nod of approval was just what Adriana needed. For good measure, she visited an astrologist, 'who told me that embroidering was absolutely perfect for me'. With expert flair, Adriana mixes stitches, ranging from the plainest to the most complicated, and alternating 2D and 3D effects. 'I can apply up to thirty stitches in one artwork,' she states. 'I usually use the finest type of thread I can get, such as antique silk. Thinner threads give a texture that contrasts with thicker threads; in the same way, unsaturated colours clash with dashes of saturated colour implemented on precise parts of the artworks.' Every one-off embroidery takes

the viewer to a whimsical destination: lions meditate while sitting on clouds; quirky cats rest in gardens; hybrid chairs sit, their backs in the form of sweaters. A spiritual dimension also hovers over some of the pieces, no doubt reflecting Adriana's interest in astrology. 'My studio is on the first floor of our house and I've collected all the tools and materials you can imagine, and I'm obsessed with being able to touch the material: I have my ascendant in Taurus after all,' she quips. 'I can also count on my creative fire, as my sun is in Leo.' The ideas of this incense-burning adept of yoga and meditation generally surface just before she goes to sleep or right before she awakes. 'First, I sketch with a pencil, and then I start making with fabric, threads or clay. When I design an object, I think of the form first and then the colour.' She has now expanded into crochet, ceramics and soft furnishings. Having been selected to represent Argentina at many international design fairs, she also teaches embroidery workshops. 'When I embroider,' she confides, 'I feel as if I have been embroidering all my life, and perhaps even in another life. I feel absolutely free.'

See also p.309
www.migadepan.com.ar

A TORRES

1. A multimedia approach: drawings and needlepoint for the 'Osvaldo Project', featuring a cute round character sporting yellow stripes (see also **8**).

2. Adriana Torres, aka Miga de Pan, is highly skilled at crochet and knitting as well as embroidery.

3. 'A Buddha and Dancing Lions with Lion Masks': an enchanting needlepoint embroidery that exudes Aztec vibes.

4. Meet 'Farnesio the Elephant', an adorable must-have in any nursery.

5. What delightful creation are these little embroidered parts going to form?

6. Adriana's workshop: a serene world of whimsical creatures and beautiful colours.

7. A tribute to Argentina and a feat of crafting: 'Giant Armadillo', made with merino wool from Patagonia, and awarded first prize at the national crafts competition organized by the Fondo Nacional de las Artes.

8. The art of composition: a ceramic 'Osvaldo' presiding over the stage.

7

8

Mister Finch

UK

Step into a subversive wonderland, where poetry arises from decay. Enchanting creatures from the animal kingdom are sewn out of salvaged fabrics. 'The inside-out of an umbrella by the side of the road could become a crow, a tattered rag on the beach a sleeping mouse. I constantly see fabrics' potential,' explains the creator of Mister Finch. Based in Leeds, Yorkshire, the eponymous 'Mister Finch' is a self-taught maker of decorative heirlooms that happy customers have adopted and made their own. 'I love the imaginative ways people have found to style them,' Finch enthuses. 'Lately I've seen my butterflies and moths *en masse*, which looked really wonderful.' A long list of lovely anecdotes reveals people falling irrationally in love with his creatures. 'A lady bought one of my spiders, but then forgot. When she opened the box, she screamed the house down and fell over. She's since bought more and admits that even she can't work out why she loves them in spite of her phobia.' Finch's inspiration comes from fairy tales, old superstitions and the natural world, especially woodland and forest environments, 'as these are what I had access to as a child', he says. 'I'd love to make something for a film – a Tim Burton would be the best!' His creations hint at Victoriana, with their fragile embroidery and engraved metal plates, as well as at primitive-style folk art through their simple lines combined with scuffed, inked materials. 'I use a lot of cotton,' Finch notes, 'so I like to add more luxurious fabrics in unexpected ways to create contrast and help set a narrative. Using velvets and silks as the linings of ears or clothing can really lift a piece.' He has been working with textiles for around five years, and now his work has evolved to become bigger, often highly exaggerated. 'I love to make really huge animals. These aren't for sale and are often projects that I work on in between pieces. The patterns are scaled-up on a projector and I look out for fabrics on my travels.' Finch works and reworks all of his patterns until he is happy with the shape. 'This then gets made up, stuffed and filled, then surface treatments from staining to dyeing and painting are applied (the earthy colour of tea pairs well with nearly every other colour). Limbs are jointed, and then I might sew on details around the face. That's when pieces really show their personalities.' These one-off revelations-come-to-life are sure to cure any creepy-crawlie phobias forever.

See also p.306
www.mister-finch.com

1. Skin-deep commitment to his art: Mister Finch holding spools of thread.

2. A glimpse of Mister Finch's desk: a gallimaufry of tools.

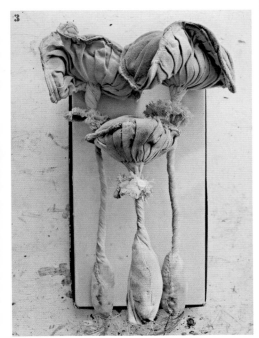

3. Fabric toadstools made with cotton and aged velvet.

4. This winsome stag beetle is made with pink velvet and cotton.

5. Alice, where are you? A benevolent giant hare, along with his spider and life-size swan companions, welcomes visitors to Mister Finch's workroom.

6. A trace of wizardry: a moth work in progress.

7. Lucky are the recipients of these moths, poised in line as if on a launch pad.

Naomi Paul

UK

The resurgence of knitting as a hobby has been well documented in recent years. At the vanguard, pre-empting the knit-kit trend, a few designers have been investigating the potential of yarn applied to contemporary living: none more so than Naomi Paul, former Young Designer of the Year (*Home & Gardens* magazine). Her holistic 'hand-knit plus homewares' creations tick all the right boxes: modern, functional, sustainable and desirable. Naomi studied graphic design at Central Saint Martins, then completed a degree in constructed textile design at Chelsea College of Art & Design. 'When I first visited Chelsea and saw the weaving room, its walls lined with coloured cones of yarn and huge cast-iron looms standing almost dinosaur-like, I knew I was in the right place,' she recalls. 'I really found my feet after working for knit designer Sid Bryan of SIBLING knitwear. He taught me so much about what it is to really understand your craft and how confidence comes through the power of knowledge.' Now Naomi's pendant lamps, chairs, floor cushions and private commissions, made using some surplus, recycled and natural materials, effortlessly enhance any interior. 'The process I use is very organic, normally starting with a material and exploring what techniques

– crochet, knit, weave, etc. – work best with its particular properties. I can then think about form. Knit and crochet can both be constructed and deconstructed quickly, so I tend to spend some time constructing and unravelling until I have the perfect form. During this time, I will also be researching and contacting as many local makers and suppliers as possible to source parts such as low-energy bulbs for my lights.' Although the products Naomi designs are a form of artistic exploration, she is fully aware that she is also growing a business. 'I have to be very conscious of designing with a purpose, while staying true to my core values.' Having grown up on a farm in Sussex, where 'make do and mend' and zero waste were a normal part of life, Naomi preserves this ethos in her work. Co-founder of the textile design collective, Bricolage, 'a think tank for sustainable, ethical, forward-thinking textile design', she is a passionate advocate of craft. 'I always try to design with emotional attachment ingrained into an object, creating a sensory experience,' she says. The more people who follow her thread, the cosier our world will be.

See also p.287
www.naomipaul.co.uk

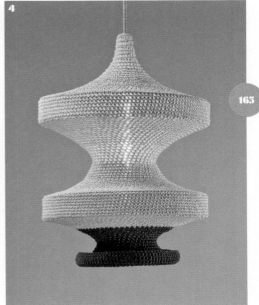

165

1. An almost-finished 'V2 Glück' pendant light occupies the floor of Naomi Paul's cosy London workshop.

2. Sculptural simplicity: a 'Glück' pendant light in navy and mustard yellow.

3. Crocheting the mercerized cotton cord.

4. Quiet opulence: a 'Sonne' pendant light in mustard yellow and navy.

5. The lustrous quality of mercerized cotton provides a luxurious touch and timelessness.

6, 7. The 'Glück' pendant light in various colour combinations and interior settings, demonstrating its versatility.

Nyholm Cantrell

Denmark

Karen Nyholm and Ned Cantrell are partners in both life and work. Married with two children, they share a studio in Aarhus. Both hot-sculpt (using a variety of techniques with hand-tools and torches to sculpt liquid glass) but they pursue two distinct paths. Ned's cheeky-looking approach is rife with social commentary. Using deceptive innocence and dark humour, his exposés are sculpted with fine details that keep them from being kitsch. 'My art is low-brow, somewhere between fine art and popular culture; often hyper-cute, yet exploring rather ugly subject matter,' he notes. 'The material and the finesse of craftsmanship are elitist and cultivated, in contrast to the ephemeral, mass-produced images from popular culture that inspire the work.' Karen, on the other hand, makes elegant statement pieces that often play on shapes and incorporate different materials, including porcelain and stainless steel. 'I see my work as aesthetically simple with a strong narrative,' she states. While different, Ned's and Karen's works are united in their sophistication, use of colour and supreme quality. Since opening their studio in 2004 ('now a vast messy creative den, since we are constantly developing new ideas,' says Karen), the pair have primarily created works for their own satisfaction, but have

nonetheless achieved resounding public success. Their medal haul includes silver and bronze at the Kunsthåndværkerprisen 1879, first prize for Ned in the KIC Prisen and the Galleri Grønlunds Hæderspris, and second prize for Karen at the GAS Student Exhibition. Ned remarks of his process, 'Often it starts with an idea of something cool that I want to try. It could be something I've seen, something historical, something material-based. I draw a lot and do tests before making the finished work with a small team of assistants: one needs a great deal of help to be able to stand alone.' He enjoys being forced to think differently when faced with restrictions and obstacles. He also finds himself working cyclically ('my skills continuously improve and my ideas become more attuned'), whereas Karen favours a steady learning curve. Ultimately, both are strong advocates of the handmade. 'Rightly or wrongly, craftsmanship is not highly valued in our society. Fortunately there exist patrons of the arts who understand its value. They play a crucial role, allowing craftsmen to take risks and make ambitious work.' The good news is that we can all be patrons.

See also p.270
www.nyholmcantrell.dk

1. Karen Nyholm opening a blown glass vessel, furnaces in the background.

2. An enchanted grove: 'Trees' in hot-sculpted glass by Karen Nyholm.

3. The duo's blackboard: an important link between initial ideas and finished pieces.

4. Graceful pink: a large, blown glass 'Acorn' vase by Karen Nyholm.

5. A blown glass 'Wink' vase by Karen Nyholm.

7

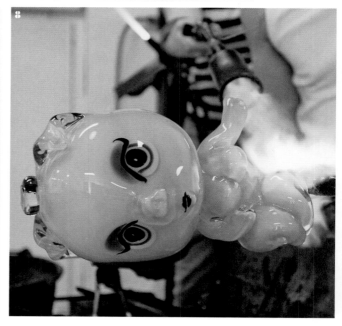

8

6, 8. Ned Cantrell and an assistant working on a prototype of 'The Little Match Girl'. Torching specific areas enables Ned to sculpt fine details.

7. Humour never goes amiss: 'Sizzling Bacon', in blown and hot-sculpted glass, by Ned Cantrell.

9

9. The best of two worlds: wooden containers with blown glass lids, by Karen Nyholm.

10. A prime example of Ned's wit: 'The Monkey as King', in blown and hot-sculpted glass, fur and velvet.

10

Oferenda Objetos

Brazil

It could be described as a happy marriage between industrial and crafty: thick crochet complementing structural metal that forms the canvas for sizeable cross-stitch interventions. The choice of hot colours points to the country of origin: Brazil. Oferenda Objetos – 'offering objects' (as gifts) – is the brainchild of Nicole Tomazi. 'I launched my company in 2007 and to begin with developed small decorative pieces. Then, in 2011, I ventured into furniture. I've always liked working with string, yarn and wire. Today I see that growth lies in drawing from my raw materials and harnessing their potential.' Nicole made the transition into design after practising as an architect. But from the moment she met designers who were self-producing and commercializing their own creations out of their own studios, it dawned on her that 'this was it!'. 'My husband is a graphic designer,' she continues, 'and both his understanding of the industry and his support were essential for me to feel safe enough to jump ahead.' Whenever Nicole has an idea, she dwells on it extensively before even putting it on paper. She maps each project in her mind, eliminating what does not work and investing in what seems worthwhile. 'When I sit down to draw, the idea is so mature in my mind that it flows onto

paper quite easily. Then I begin the experiments, prototypes and tests. The idea is so defined that I don't make many changes from the first draft to the final piece.' She explains, 'I like to fall in love with the idea. I think about it all the time, cherishing it. By the time I turn it into mini prototypes, it has become a rabid passion!' This level of involvement explains why Nicole sees each creation as an extension of her heart and soul, and why she is so keen to see an emotional connection triggered in the public. 'The product must "say something". When I did the "Fractal" collection, for instance, I sought the texture of broccoli for textiles; I never imagined this would urge so many people to touch and feel the pieces. The same goes with my "Raft" series: people reported they felt they had been transported to the beach. Feeling always goes beyond what the piece represents,' she enthuses. Ultimately Nicole would like to increase her production capacity. In keeping with her striving for authenticity, comfort and functionality, she would also love to design a bicycle. Useful, touching and fun: bywords for Oferenda Objetos.

See also p.263
www.oferenda.net
www.nicoletomazi.com

1, 3. Nicole Tomazi puts her ideas down in a notebook. Her creations are an integral part of her working environment.

2. Bold and beautiful: a 'Floppy' vase in polyester rope, from the 'Jangada' collection.

4. A cross-pollination of ideas comes from sharing a studio – an ample, bright space within a refurbished old house – with a jewelry designer and a clothing designer.

5. The 'Fractal' table, made with polyester rope crochet and a stainless steel frame.

6

9. **9.** 'Land in sight, captain': the 'Jangada' stool, chair and multipurpose wall panel could soon be reaching your home.

7

8

6. Needlepoint on a massive scale: working on a 'Jangada' seat with yellow polyester rope.

7. Handmade with surplus crochet fabric, the 'Granny Judith' chair from the 'Granny's Industry' collection has more than one trick up its sleeve.

8. Polyester ropes in a vivid palette of primary colours.

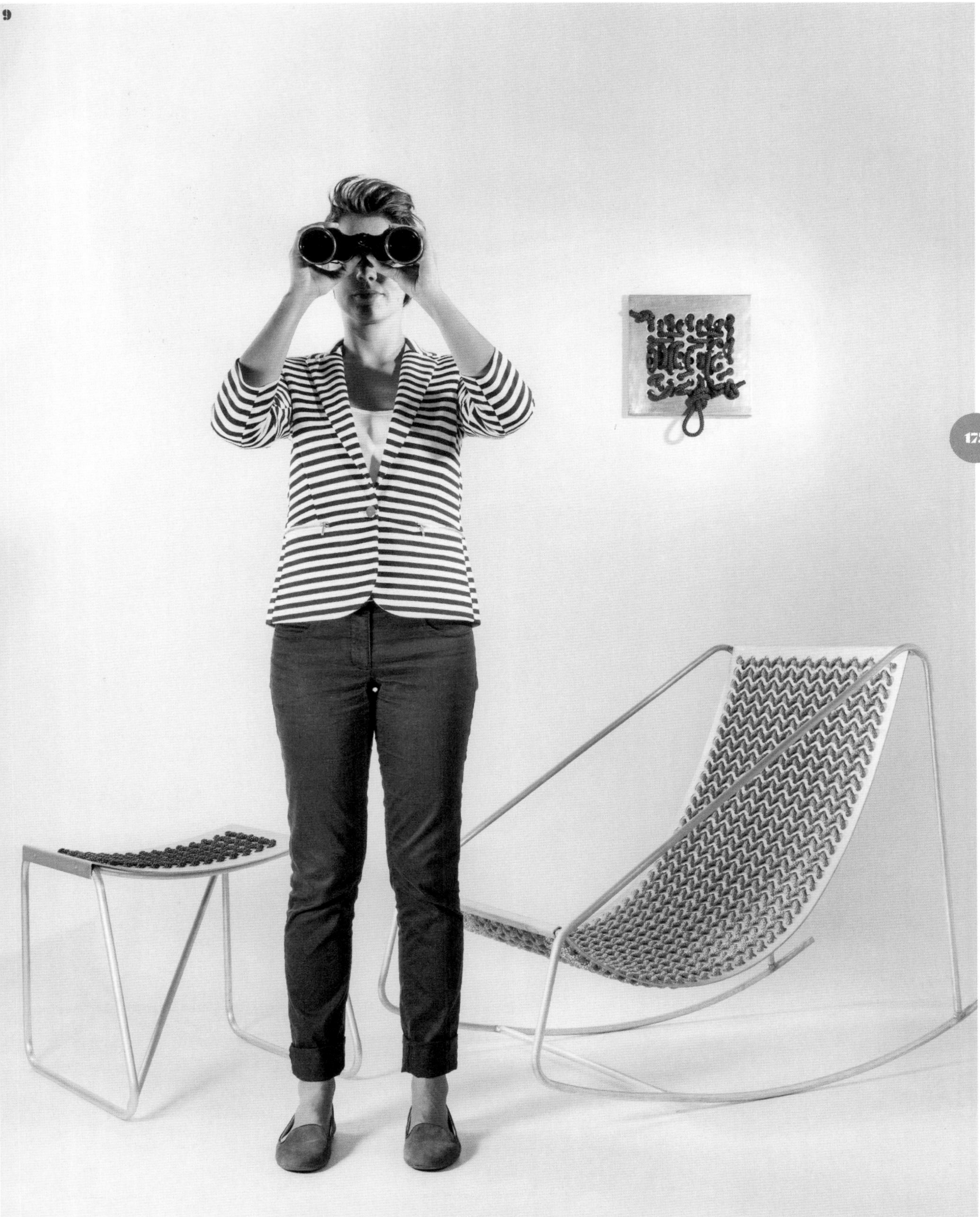

Paper-Cut-Project

USA

What was once a flat sheet is now an awe-inspiring couture showpiece. Behind the scenes, like a designer constructing a garment in toile, is the sketching, measuring, cutting, curling and gluing of paper. There is something undeniably sartorial about Paper-Cut-Project's creations; indeed, its co-founders, Nikki Nye and Amy Flurry, focus primarily on headdresses, wigs, masks and accessories. 'We only use paper, glue and a finish coat. The unusual thing is how we make the paper behave. That's our "secret sauce".' Nikki is the paper-sculpting maestro. She has a BFA in interior design, 'but running my own business – a fashion/lifestyle boutique called Addiction – was what helped me to realize that there needs to be some form of practicality behind it all if you really want something to work as a career and not just as a hobby'. Amy, in turn, brings a fine sensibility that is in tune with high fashion's appetite for visual theatrics. 'My previous career as a fashion editor and freelance writer led me to write for magazines, produce features and work with photographers for over fifteen years. For magazine shoots there's always the element of storytelling, and to do this visually you might need to create things that don't already exist.' Paper-Cut-Project evolved out of a fanciful idea over dinner

one night: to decorate a store window in their hometown Atlanta, 'a city where there wasn't a whole lot of emphasis on windows and their visual direction. We wanted to counter the movement of fast fashion with something one-of-a-kind and handmade. We chose paper as our signature because Nikki had been working with it for her own art since college. It took a few months for the boutique we approached – Jeffrey – to give us the green light. When they did, they reported that they wanted us to install paper wigs at both their Atlanta *and* New York locations.' When Amy's husband finally saw the completed creations, he exclaimed, 'Those aren't props, they're art!' Paper-Cut-Project have since been rewarded by many prestigious collaborations: masks for Hermès in Paris, wigs for the V&A Museum in London, working with super-stylist Giovanna Battaglia; 'being featured in the *New York Times* was pretty cool, too'. The low-key nature of their operation – just the two of them at work – guarantees exclusivity. 'The fact that we continue to find new ways to manipulate paper is a source of constant joy.' For us as well as for them.

See also p.294
www.paper-cut-project.com

3

3. Marie-Antoinette would faint with envy: a monumental headpiece with curls and butterflies, made as part of an exclusive collection for RED Valentino.

4. A cut-out butterfly visits its birthplace: the all-white palette of the paper conveys depth through shadows.

1. A chain reaction: sketching, tracing and cutting out immaculate white paper shapes.

2. Delicate butterflies waiting to adorn a headpiece.

5, 6. Majestic paper masks: a 'Great Horn Ram' and a 'Cockatiel', two of thirty animal masks created exclusively for Hermès.

7. Precision with a scalpel: the deft touch of a maker.

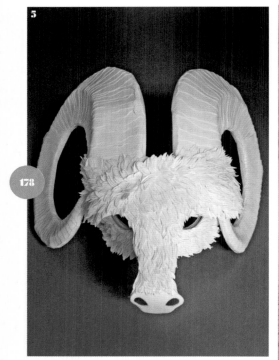

8. The belle of the ball: this paper headpiece is now part of a private collection.

Papier à Êtres

France

A duet also makes a hand-quartet, but in this case the theme is not music but a different kind of lyricism – the fashioning of paper lamps into poetic sculptures, or sculpted poems: principal characters in their own narratives. This is inscribed in the company name, Papier à êtres®: from paper (the source material) to beings (the eventual creations). 'I mainly use papier-mâché, and only in white,' says co-founder Sophie Mouton-Perrat. 'The noise paper makes when it's ripped, the textural differences between each type of paper: it's a highly sensual material to us.' Fellow founder Frédéric Guibrunet adds, 'Pleating the pre-glued paper is very tactile, and then the way in which the light interacts with the finished creation is a highly visual affair.' Sophie studied applied arts at the École Estienne and synthetic materials at ENSAAMA in Paris, and has worked with paper for some twenty years. Frédéric committed to paper a little later, in 1999. After studying chemistry at university, he worked for various pharmaceutical and cosmetics laboratories, where he was exposed to paper as a compound. 'I discovered it through its chemistry,' he confirms, 'namely the cellulose that exists in most plant fibres.' This led him to start experimenting with papier-mâché, all the while pursuing his interest in learning about paper-making. 'I travelled a lot in Southeast Asia, Europe and North America, looking for paper-manufacturing workshops,' he recalls. Both he and Sophie now consider themselves artists/artisans in the Art Décoratif or Arts and Crafts sense. 'The "handmade" fascinates us due to the fact that there will always be slight variations, even though repetitive gestures are applied.' Their 'Mademoiselle' lamp, a graceful sylph whose balloon skirt warmly glows, captures a delicate sense of movement, while their 'Dans les Branches' ceiling light offers a playful scene with a Lilliputian perched on one side counterbalancing a baby elephant hanging from its trunk on the other. 'The key is to remain curious and to charge ahead,' the pair proclaim. Keen supporters have included the Paris-based Galerie Talents (Atelier d'Art de France) and Galerie de l'Opéra de Paris, as well as the Musée des Arts Décoratifs for whom Sophie and Frédéric designed a window display. Each Papier à êtres® creation, using only environmentally friendly paper, PH-neutral glues and LED bulbs, is as gentle on the planet as it is on the soul.

See also p.284
www.papieraetres.com

4. Frédéric positioning 'Mademoiselle' lamps (or is he eavesdropping?).

5. The 'Dans les Branches' pendant light exudes poetry and sparks the imagination.

6. Home sweet home: the 'Cabanon Duo' lamp aglow.

6

1. Building the 'Mademoiselle' lamp is a meticulous process that involves very gentle handling.

2. Frédéric Guibrunet gluing paper around the metal frame of a 'Cabanon' lamp.

3. Papier-mâché heaven: works at different stages stored floor-to-ceiling in the duo's workshop.

Polly Burton

UK

The women in Polly Burton's family seem to be the custodians of creativity: her mother trained as an upholsterer and made her daughters toys, clothes and dolls' outfits when they were little ('she also kitted out our ambulance-turned-camper van with cushions, bedding and curtains'). Her grandmother, in turn, was an antique dealer of sorts, who amassed a vast collection of textiles and trimmings, 'most not particularly valuable, but interesting and beautiful. I remember looking through her chests of drawers filled with fabric and haberdashery: silks from the 1930s and prints from the 1950s and '60s.' After seeing a Louise Bourgeois exhibition, showing exquisite collages the artist had made with fabric from her parents' textile factory, Polly felt compelled to make her own collages using her grandmother's legacy. Having started off working in admin in the BBC's film department, she realized she wanted to do something creative that fitted in with family life. 'I met a friend who had just started a textile foundation course, so I enrolled on the same course, then went on to do a degree in textiles at Chelsea College of Art & Design.' Polly decided to dedicate herself to producing hand-printed fabrics. 'Artist/designer/artisan: I relate to all three at different stages of the process

– artist in the early drawing phase, working with a variety of mediums, sometimes combined with stencils; designer when turning drawings into workable designs, playing around with the composition of different elements; and artisan when transferring my designs to screen, often pinning out several pieces of cloth at once and printing and overprinting.' Nature is ever-present in Polly's designs, and indeed her studio overlooks her garden ('I love finding different plant/flower shapes and colours that work well together'). She likes to use fabrics that have minimal environmental impact, such as hemp; 'I also love dyeing silk and have used acid dyes which give great colours'. Some of her designs are sold as samples and others are used for tea towels, cushions and chair coverings. 'I think it's the element of surprise that is so wonderful, and knowing that no two pieces are the same,' she muses. 'As a general rule buying something that's more costly saves in the long-term, as it's likely it's been better designed and made, and the buyer will have thought more about the purchase and it's therefore less likely to end up in landfill.' Proof positive!

See also p.312
www.pollyburton.co.uk

5

187

6

1. Polly Burton screen-printing.

2. Haberdashery neatly stored in boxes makes for a kaleidoscopic sight.

3. Polly's hallmark of elegance is markedly diverse in inspiration: 'Geometric', 'Starfish' and 'Seaweed' prints.

4. Trials and studies, all with a calligraphic quality.

5. Polly's prints are a great way to spruce up 1950s furniture, or any for that matter.

6. Chromatic depth at its best: a 'Stitch Print' cushion in blue silk.

Renata Meirelles

Brazil

Who would have thought dissection could produce such wonders? In this case, the cutting is of raw textile surfaces into gossamer-thin shawls, jewelry and wall panels. The textiles are painstakingly worked down to their core fibres, exposing their precious fragility and extreme fluidity. 'I really love to watch the transformation of ideas into objects; the alchemy of making,' explains Renata Meirelles. 'I like to think of myself as a creator and of my works as the creatures.' Each one-of-a-kind composition has a 'second skin' quality. Complementing this, Renata operates in a totally sustainable way. 'I aim at combining industrial and handcraft techniques, featuring complete use of the given material to achieve zero waste. What is left over from one laser-cutting process may be used in another. This is the secret behind sustainability, and it has become an essential part of my creative process for brainstorming new pieces.' Renata studied visual arts at FAAP in São Paulo, then worked in the product development of stationery and leather accessories, and also in graphic design. 'My mother was a visual artist and always encouraged me in that direction. At the age of 10, I was already enrolled in a school for painting,' recalls Renata. 'At university, I hand-made pieces for my day-to-day life, such as business cards. Once I finished university, at the age of 20, I was invited to participate in a design fair to present my cards, folders and diaries, made out of paper and textiles and enhanced with watercolours and engravings. Then I developed a small line of products and received a lot of orders.' In 1995, Renata started using laser-cutting, which she first applied to steel and paper. Five years later, she moved on to laser-cutting light textiles such as silk and has not looked back since. She has garnered many prestigious commissions along the way, including work for a Brazilian film producer and for O2 Films, as well as her first large-format panels for the Brazilian Design Biennale ('a major challenge; the outcome emulated a giant textile waterfall'). Renata's wildest dream would be 'to have a piece in every country abroad!' Her customers often buy an item for themselves, and then return to buy another as a gift. 'Several have told me that they are even stopped in the street by people wanting to touch the piece and asking where they got it from.' Renata's compelling creations speak for themselves.

See also p.275
www.renatameirelles.net

1. Renata Meirelles reviewing a fabric that has just been laser-cut.

2. '4M' and 'CIR' polyester panels come in a myriad of contrasting colours.

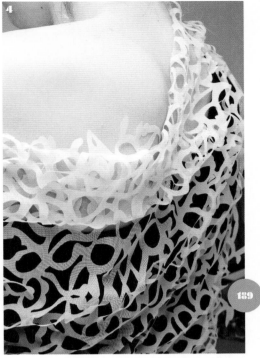

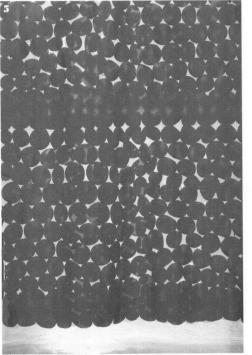

189

3. Each one is unique: '4M' and 'CIR' panels of leather cord and taffeta, from the 'Score Family' collection.

4, 7. Like a second skin: 'REN 8X' polyester shawls in white and black.

5. The magical filtering of light: this '4M' polyester panel can work as a curtain or a room divider.

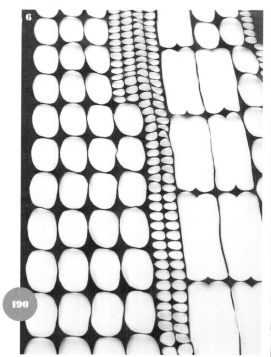

6. Negative cut-outs of adhesive taffetas, from the 'Velaturas' and 'Score Family' collections.

8. Examples of negative and positive cut-outs of adhesive taffetas, 'Velaturas' and 'Score Family' collections.

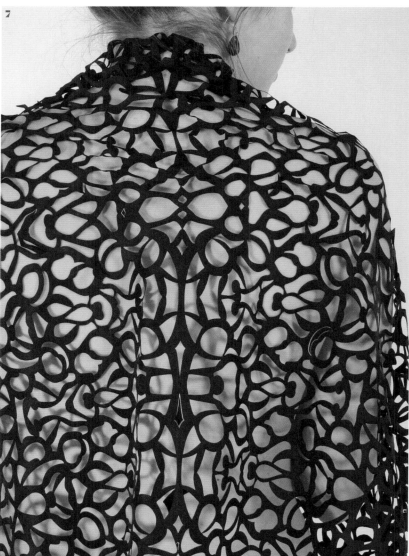

9. So delicate it seems to float: a detail of the 'Score' shawl in silk cord and taffeta.

10. A necklace or scarf to complement any neckline: the 'CIR 138' in taffeta.

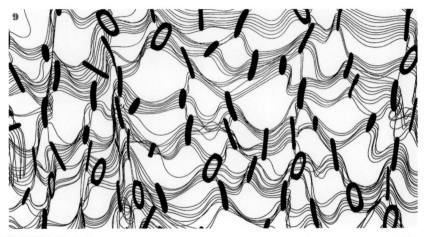

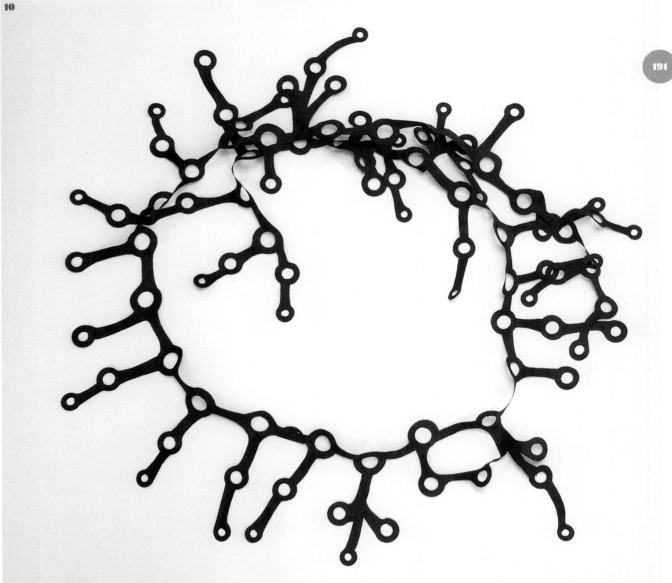

Res Anima

Germany

'We strive to create timeless products that combine contemporary design, traditional craftsmanship and poetry,' proclaim Ina Woelk and Philipp Hinderer, aka Res Anima. 'Only a fraction of the thousands of objects that are produced, used and disposed of are ever truly revered, loved and missed. We believe that well-made objects can slowly take root in their owners' heart. Every object we make is geared to that idea.' Ina and Philipp decided to pursue apprenticeships as carpenters, having, unbeknownst to each other, graduated from the same secondary school. Ina joined the institute for woodwork and design in Garmisch-Partenkirchen, and Philipp the master school for carpenters in Munich. They both went on to study industrial design at the Academy of Fine Arts in Stuttgart, where they finally met. 'We've always worked with different materials, as we're keen to expand our knowledge of substances and manufacturing techniques. However, we've discovered a clear preference for natural materials – wood, clay, bronze – which somehow have magical energy properties,' the pair state. 'Turning a raw piece of material into a beautiful object with your own hands is for us one of the most fascinating aspects of craftsmanship. This means more than just shaping the outer shell; it means giving an object its substance and soul.' The pair start by drawing, making small models or simply experimenting with their chosen materials. 'We usually try to combine traditional handcraft with state-of-the-art methods of development and design. This helps us to get a lot of full-size preliminary models very quickly. Producing 3D data simultaneously allows us to verify our draft and to shape it very precisely. We believe that putting high emphasis on materials and their processing, as well as on the functionality of every single detail, makes the difference between unique, crafted design objects and soulless plastic moulds.' The duo value time as an ally ('good things need time') and place great importance on ethical trading standards ('we would never use tropical wood or cheap leather from China: it's not about making expensive luxury goods, it's about making good products'). As the German saying goes: 'Schreiner sehen mit ihren Händen' (carpenters see with their hands). With Res Anima's finely balanced, honest and durable products, we receive a beautiful demonstration of this.

See also p.262
www.resanima.de

1. Introducing Ina Woelk and Philipp Hinderer, aka Res Anima.

2. Cylindrical wooden rods used in the construction process.

3. A family portrait: 'Hockl', the three-legged stool with a chair back, in ash; 'Schmuck', the flower choker in cast bronze; 'Seidla', the half-litre mug in earthenware; and 'Muk', the cherished dachshund in soft loden.

4. Raw wooden slabs take shape under the machine saw.

5. An early stage of 'Hockl', the stool that will become a chair.

6

7

195

8

6. 'Prost!' This 'Seidla' beer mug is Res Anima's tribute to their national heritage.

7. A soft colour palette is key to the company's signature style.

8. Every wooden slat is individually labelled.

Rosemary Milner

UK

With her 'heirlooms for sentiment', Rosemary Milner invites us to pay homage to British heritage. Her work explores the flora and fauna of her native countryside through a combination of traditional techniques such as embroidery, copper etching and linoprint, and found objects such as pressed flowers ('for the aesthetic of the velvety, delicate petals in among the etching compositions of animals and birds') or original correspondence found at antique markets ('sometimes in French, which creates an air of mystery that chimes in perfectly with my practice'). Rosemary maintains a connection to her roots through lengthy country walks: 'the bleak, windswept North Yorkshire moors and the meadow clifftops of Saltburn are my favourite spots for natural inspiration'. Historically, the Tudor and Victorian periods have always been of special interest to her, and she likes to visit stately homes. 'The stories from these historic landmarks and the way people used to live are an essential starting point in my creative and conceptual processes. Once the theme of my historical narrative starts flowing, I can piece together the imagery.' Rosemary makes use of upcycling to create a nostalgic aesthetic, embroidering onto old linens and lace, thus reinforcing her historical themes since her

materials already hold a story through their age. 'I like to imagine where my fabrics have been to explain why there's a small tear or a maker's mark. Keeping the original features of the cloth is very important. I also use a lot of old envelopes and postcards, and I love the idea that someone viewing my wallpapers or embroidery can look closely enough to see the writing and read all the different stories.' Rosemary practised criss-cross stitching as a young girl but only really began to master embroidery after an elective in her second year of university. Now her most impressive techniques are the daisy and leaf stitches. She also experiments with print processes to create interesting effects. Once she has figured out which techniques work effectively together, she often carries the method through each medium in a collection, with slight variations for each item. 'For me, the finishing touches are what create a good piece: beautiful stitchery, scraps of lace… It's the same with the final flourish of tatters of letters and stamps on my wallpaper.' With her age-old printing presses and her upcycling, Rosemary's products are charmingly holistic.

See also p.307
www.rosemary-milner.co.uk

3

1. Poetic touches here and there in the workshop.

2. The big reveal: Rosemary Milner lifting a print after it has been passed through the etching press.

3. A 'Willow Blue Tit' etching and embroidery on a found handkerchief. Embroidery – 'portable, beautiful, and above all adding a wonderful, delicate texture to my etching pieces' – is Rosemary's favourite technique.

4, 6. Messy fun: inking printing plates with thick etching ink.

4

7. The copper plates have been inked and already one can see the detailed birds coming to life.

8. A 'Tree Sparrow' card featuring a hand-drawn illustration in fine liner and watercolour on 100% recycled stock, from the 'Willow Bank' collection.

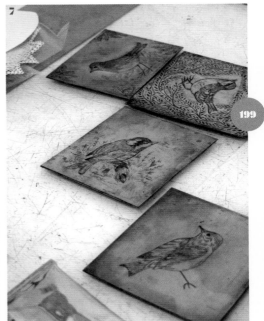

199

5. A jack of all crafts! Painting, embroidery, printmaking and etching: Rosemary's talents are manifold.

Sally Nencini

UK

Sally Nencini fizzes with excitement as she points out her embroidered chairs and her homewares bedecked with joyous motifs. 'I just do what makes me happy. I love working with colour and fabric, making beautiful objects to use and look at. I hope this gives other people some pleasure, too.' Sally started learning the art of upholstery in 2003, and knitting in 2008, although she had touched upon this at art college; she was never taught embroidery but has long been a practitioner. 'I like seeing something evolve, when it's down to me how it will look as a finished piece. With upholstery, it's so satisfying starting from something that may seem broken and beyond repair then turning it into a useful and unique object.' Sally was taught to sew by her mother. 'Much of the inspiration for my knits comes from childhood memories: the cloth-kit clothes my mum used to make, the old wooden puzzles and picture card games. I still love fabrics and toys from the 1960s and earlier.' Many of Sally's embroidery ideas stem from nature and her surroundings: trees, leaves, shadows and textures. When upholstering, Sally begins with the piece of furniture, trusting that its shape will inspire a design or type of stitch. She often sews straight onto the cover or else uses a rough pencil outline. 'I've also worked with my husband, Peter Nencini, on a number of embroidered furniture commissions,' she notes. 'There may be a family chair passed down through generations or from a particular place of meaning to the owner. Peter will take the information, do research, then work on a surface design. We talk through stitches and colours, then Peter screen-prints the outline of the design onto the cover for me to stitch.' Sally mainly uses backgrounds of natural linen ('I feel it's the perfect colour to offset a stitch and colour'). However, the lengthy processes involved might explain why she has taken up machine-knitting alongside her other work ('there's an instant result,' she admits). Her latest creation is a range of poufs and stools. 'I found recycled cardboard tubes to form the inside of the poufs; for the stools I re-used the legs from vintage furniture.' The beauty of Sally's work lies in its careful reference to personal history. Each object carries – or holds the promise of carrying – particular memories and stories, like an old friend. Isn't that what matters most? Surrounding ourselves with meaningful possessions for a lifetime and beyond.

See also pp. 305, 311
www.sallynencini.com

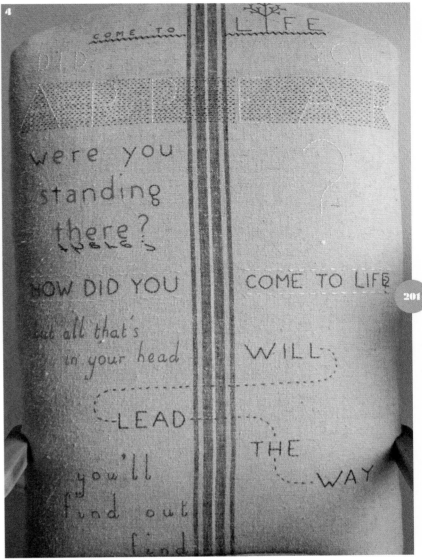

1. Sally Nencini at her sewing machine.

2. A stitching detail from the 'Mayo' chair: the embroidery, upholstery and design are all testament to Sally's skills.

3. How inviting! The 'Mayo' chair, with a mid-century frame: upholstery, embroidery and design created by Sally.

4, 5. The embroidery and upholstery of the 'Come to Life' chair are by Sally; the type design is by her husband; the words were written by their then-eight-year-old daughter.

6. Sally sewing a knitted fabric.

7. Children love the 'Fairisle Dolly', made of knitted lambswool. 'I've made her many times now, but she still makes me happy!' says Sally.

8. Having a well-deserved break: Sally in her studio in an old, disused factory in Peckham, south London.

9. As gorgeous on their own as they are stacked: 'Tulip and Daisy' cushions in knitted lambswool.

10. Equipped to unleash their creativity: knitted lambswool 'DRAW' pencil bags for children (and grown-up children).

203

Savo&Pomelina

Belgium

It took a holiday on a Greek island for Eva Craenhals truly to affirm the fact that 'making' was a vital pillar for her happiness. 'I'd been worrying about how to justify what I do; or whether I should go down a new path and, if so, which…until I happened to go into a little shop with an olive tree in front, some jazz playing in the background, wine and cheese on a table, and there in the middle a man making exquisite pottery: the very picture of peace,' Eva recalls. 'People such as this craftsman are my heroes.' Back home in Ghent, Eva's own creative energies whirl at high speed. 'Pictures and visions engulf me. I have to be very sharp and make choices, throwing elements away until nothing but the product remains.' Having established herself as a multidisciplinary designer and maker, she can fill literally any space, from floor to ceiling, each product a consistent element in a comprehensive decorative vision. 'Whatever I make somehow radiates in the same manner. I have a typical way of using colours, materials and space,' she notes. Her sleek furniture blends with graphic cushions in a signature palette of cherry red, slate blue and moss green or oversized anatomical organs made out of felt. Her repertoire encapsulates a poetic and playfully elegant statement. 'Artisanal handwriting combined with industrial production methods and room for imagination' is how she describes her style. She studied art at the Industrial Design Academy in Eindhoven, before moving to Indonesia for a couple of years. On her return, she designed for a large-volume textile company: 'it was challenging to create for such a wide group of people; to please them while also pleasing myself, consistently creating with clearly defined materials and goals'. Following the birth of her daughter, Eva founded Savo&Pomelina 'to make objects that I thought would make a nicer world'. 'Good designs are like vibrations,' she adds. 'It's not only about the product; it's about its relationship to its surroundings.' Expert at snatching time in her busy life to get things done, Eva fantasizes about creating a wooden hotel for children, an ice cream truck, a tree house, a collection of paper dresses, a theme park, and 'always more simple-hearted objects; three-dimensional poetry'. She often feels overwhelmed at the end of a big project, but nevertheless concludes, 'I get so blocked that the only way out is by making. And then it starts all over again!'

See also pp. 266, 315
www.savopomelina.be

1. 'Look into my eye!' Eva Craenhals presenting her 'Pouf Eye' floor cushion in woollen felt.

2. Woollen felt 'Hand' sculptures, with embroidery.

3. Scanning the room: 'Eyeballs' in small and medium sizes, from the 'Enter' collection.

4. A series of preparatory prints for fronts and backs of cushions in the 'Fudge' range.

5. A cheerful 'Closet Tumble' made of beech, plywood, print, linoleum and leather, from the 'Acrobat' collection.

6. The Savo&Pomelina showroom looks like a modern interpretation of a medieval banquet hall.

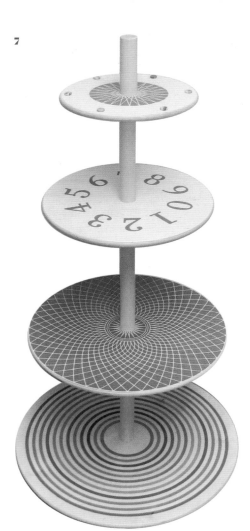

7. Playfulness is paramount in Eva's work. The jolly 'Étagère' in printed plywood and beech looks like a giant cake stand.

8. Filling in an 'Eyeball' with felted white wool.

207

Sebastian Cox

UK

Strolling through woodlands in Kent, you might stumble upon a young man harvesting coppiced hazels, absorbing the sensory delights offered by birdsong and the sweet smell of cut wood. That would be Sebastian Cox, the British woodworker/designer and advocate of sustainability, once described by Kevin McCloud of the TV programme *Grand Designs* as a 'true adventurer'. 'One of my ambitions,' Sebastian declares, 'is to raise awareness of the beauty of British hardwoods and to encourage consumers in the UK to value home-grown ash, sycamore, lacewood, chestnut and so on.' The challenges posed by his chosen material only spur him on. 'When we bossy humans try to manipulate wood with sophisticated tools, it still does what it wants! All we can do is treat it well and try to understand it to get the best results from it.' The apple has not fallen far from the tree. Sebastian's father runs a company that restores timber-framed buildings, and the young man's fate was further sealed when his maternal grandfather presented him with 'my great-grandfather's set of rebate block planes. He was a carpenter. The tools were a little rusty but very beautiful. I spent some time restoring them, and now use them when needed.' After studying furniture design and craftsmanship, followed by

design at Masters level, Sebastian realized that he could make a career 'inventing' things, thereby following a childhood dream. He now thinks up designs, usually while doing the repetitive job of milling timber. 'Then I'll perhaps put pen to paper, or pencil to clean-bit-of-workbench, and scribble something down. I can either turn to CAD or a mock-up to begin to work out form and proportions. I return to the workbench to make the piece. I like to see it life-size and to get a feel for it as soon as possible.' Honesty – whether in materials (showing blemishes and grain patterns) or construction (showing how a piece is made or held together) – is Sebastian's watchword. He also has a particular fondness for the dovetail joint, 'a beautifully logical way to assemble two pieces of wood…and there's nothing more satisfying than a neat fit on the first try'. His customers – who include Liberty department store and Heal's lifestyle chain – would surely agree when Sebastian points out, 'Genuine beauty can be timeless if the right doses of elegance, proportion, simplicity, detail, craftsmanship and texture are included.'

See also pp. 260, 285
www.sebastiancox.co.uk

3

1. Sebastian Cox polishing a 'Suent Superlight' chair with care and pride.

2. An interesting contrast between modern computer-aided graphics and the rustic aspects of the workshop.

4

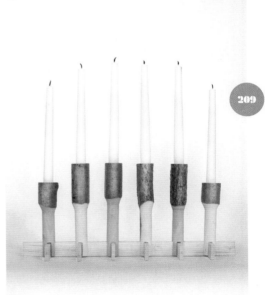

209

5

3. The bowler hat makes the 'Brish' hat stand in coppiced hazel quintessentially British, but the fine design makes it universal.

4. 'Lop & Top' candelabra: an astute construction number with a comely look.

5. A furniture reunion: the 'Suent Superlight' chair, 'Rod' desk lamp, 'Lop & Top' candelabra and 'Rod' standard lamp, all from the 'Silviculture' series, share a family resemblance.

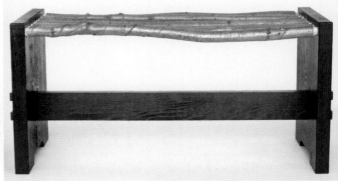

6. The line between woodland and workshop blurs organically: here, Sebastian is working on a 'Kerf' stool/side table.

7. A natural pairing of a 'Rod' standard lamp and a 'Suent Superlight' chair in grey.

8, 10. Form and function: the 'Pole' bench, in coppiced hazel, from the 'Silviculture' series.

9. Lean in: the 'Rod' desk lamp in coppiced hazel.

211

Suna Fujita

Japan

Here is something ravishing to behold: a palm-sized ceramic sculpture, portraying a mystical wonderland of benevolent symbiosis. 'We hope to evoke an ideal world in which animals and humans live together,' confirm husband-and-wife team, Shohei Fujita and Chisato Yamano, aka Suna Fujita. 'The most distinctive elements of our work are painting and decoration. We make sure we don't adopt any traditional designs or existing patterns.' The pair hope that the durability of ceramics means that their works will 'be loved by people who are alive a hundred years from now'. 'That's why we paint animals on our vessels,' they add. 'We want to leave images of the nature of our time. Since our environment is in a critical condition and many species are becoming extinct every day, it's possible that the animals we paint won't exist in the future. People might only learn that there were once creatures like these from our works. The works can therefore act as a kind of barometer for looking at ourselves.' The couple are, however, careful to tackle their fears with a cheerful heart. 'We want to express a joyful and happy world because the most important goal of our creations is to make people who see and use our works have a joyful and happy time.' Whether a piece is purely artistic or utilitarian –

a sake flask, say, a candy pot, a spouted cup or a goblet – it displays multilayered images through an interactive use of *mitate* (the Japanese concept of likening one thing to another). Onlookers are invited to use their imagination. The more one delves into the fantasy, the more optimistic one ends up feeling. 'We've been working with ceramics for ten years,' the pair share. 'Recently it's taken us longer to complete pieces because they're becoming more substantial and intensive.' Once an idea is agreed, Shohei generally forms the shape of the vessel, while Chisato takes charge of the painting. 'Scratching with needles, applying slipware and scraping it off create the patterns on the surface. Lastly, we fire the piece. Most of the materials and techniques we use are orthodox, but our ways of combining them may be unusual.' Shohei and Chisato are fascinated by the connection between their creations and the people who own them. 'In the case of tableware, for example, our works can actually make people's dining experience more enjoyable,' they enthuse. The pair's delight is shared.

See also p.255
http://blog.goo.ne.jp/fujitachisato
www.artcourtgallery.com

1. Welcome to the home of Shohei Fujita and Chisato Yamano in the city of Imabari, Ehime Prefecture.

2. Chisato at work in the bright, airy main room of her home/studio.

3. Look closely at this tale of friendship shown on the 'Beaver Nest' pot with lid (*futamono*), made in wheel-thrown porcelain, painted with coloured slip and overglazed.

4

214

5

4. Auspicious black birds soar above children having fun on the 'Sunset' sake flask (*tokkuri*).

5. Jungle Eden: a 'Tapir Mother and Child' *futamono* in wheel-thrown pottery.

6. The designs are so delicate that Shohei has to use a deft touch at the potter's wheel.

7. Delineating the illustrations is an opportunity to delve deep into an enchanting world.

8. A testimony to the duo's boundless imagination: assorted small plates in wheel-thrown pottery, painted with coloured slip.

6

Susan Hipgrave

Australia

Victorian ornithologists and botanists would have heartily commended Susan Hipgrave's remarkable series of hand-painted plates. The meticulous execution (each extra-fine brushstroke adding an important detail), the resulting life-like renditions and the consistent format (monochromatic black on white; identical one-size ceramic plates) adhere to the ethos of scientific study. Susan's ability to focus is well matched by her possession of a steady hand. However, it soon becomes clear that all is not quite as it seems. Susan departs from a straightforward replication of flora and fauna by concocting strange hybrids or by exaggerating features, such as piercing eyes to convey the extreme visual acuity of an eagle. For spectators, an interactive experience awaits: birds, caught in the moment, watch us, ready to strike or to fly away; clusters of twisted vines and treacherous spikes draw us in. 'As my work with natural subjects becomes more detailed, so my subjects become more assertive,' the artist states. 'When I'm contemplating a new piece, I start by going through my collection of natural history books until I find something that "speaks" to me. I work with it in terms of size and placement, and then begins the slow and meditative practice of putting paint to porcelain. I obsess about how

fine a line I can do; ultimately, I love seeing all the little black lines that I've painted come together to create an image.' Despite the striking maturity of her work, Susan has been working in ceramic art for less than a decade. For many years she worked as an art director/designer in advertising. Then, in 2005, 'sick with shingles, I walked into a shop that was running ceramic painting classes and it was immediately obvious that it was something I had to do'. While she has worked with earthenware as well as porcelain, her medium has always been the plate. 'My art is contained, so I can pack it up and travel easily,' Susan notes. 'We have a house on the south coast, so I spend much of my time there, painting in daylight.' Her creations work well both on a small scale (a single plate) and a large scale (her first exhibition – a strikingly spectacular window display at the GRANTPIRRIE gallery in Sydney – showcased several plates placed against a dark backdrop). If there were an issue with Susan's hand-painted works, it would be that once you have admired one, you compulsively want to collect them all.

See also p.249
www.susanhipgrave.com

3

1. Victorian-style ornithology revived: a 'Mare Aquila – Sea Eagle' plate.

2. Susan Hipgrave browsing through her shelves of inspirational books.

4

5

3. A 'Cytinus Hypocistus' plate: the painstakingly detailed illustration appears almost 3D, thanks to a precise accumulation of light/dark lines and shadows.

4. Susan's works have great impact when grouped: (from top to bottom) 'Brugmansis', 'Cytinus Hypocistus', 'Asclepiad' and 'Parasitic Balaphoreae' plates.

5. A black and white affair: an inspirational botanical drawing, a container holding extra-fine brushes and a pot of black ink.

6. Susan's artworks add drama to any wall: (clockwise from left) 'Nest of European Jay', 'Eolophus Roseicapilla – Roseate Cockatoo' and 'Arara – Brazilian Macaw' plates.

7. Susan at work in her exquisitely appointed Sydney home.

Takashi Tomii

Japan

We often wonder how we can improve our everyday lives. What if the things we own had the ability to help us? Take Takashi Tomii's wooden utensils, tableware and furniture: everyday, utilitarian objects whose simplicity is sublime. 'I would be very happy if I could always love what I touch when I cook, eat, and so on. I think that is what artisans can achieve by making things they really feel passionate about,' muses Takashi. Having been inspired by the foresting industry he saw as a high school student during a year spent in Vernonia, Oregon, he eventually set up his own workshop in Japan in 2008. 'At first I was eager to make special things that couldn't be found anywhere else. However, this shifted. I now want to make things that are so simple and ordinary that I can automatically identify my touch in any of my pieces.' Takashi originally majored in applied physics – one of his heroes is still Richard P. Feynman, 'who made me aware of how wonderful this universe is, and how tiny a being I am' – and he recognizes that 'the years I was addicted to scientific studies strongly affected my way of thinking, which eventually made me into the maker I am today'. His workshop in Minamiyamashiro, Kyoto, is a hive of projects, always accomplished with care and expertise,

but one criterion predominates: he only makes objects he would like to own and use in everyday life. 'The process is like simplifying a mathematical equation into the shortest and most meaningful form. Since my shapes are usually very simple, I don't draw anything before making. I generally start with a board, sometimes a log, and make it into a shape with the help of machinery and hand-tools. One shave can make things look totally different, so it's always enjoyable to decide when to stop shaving.' He finishes his pieces with either natural oil or *urushi*, a traditional Japanese lacquer. 'Bringing out the beauty of the wood – mostly chestnut, cherry, oak and birch – is important for me.' His ambition is to democratize Japanese woodwork, which includes exporting and exhibiting internationally (his first overseas show – at the Mjölk Gallery in Toronto – received rave reviews). One idea is to stage a food event at which his tableware is used. 'This kind of trial is very popular in Japan,' he shares, 'letting people feel that works made by craftsmen are "better", more attractive and more charming than mass-produced pieces.' We could not agree more.

See also p.300
www.takashitomii.com

4

1. Takashi Tomii turning the bottom of a dish.

2. Shaping the rim of a hand-carved birch bowl with a spokeshave.

3. A tribute to the material of which they are made: this series of petal dishes comes in cherry or chestnut wood, finished with oil or *urushi*.

5

4. Less is more: hand-carved and turned bowls, finished with natural oil.

5. Oh so divine, oh so Japanese: a series of cherrywood sake cups, finished with white *urushi*.

6. Carving the inside of a chestnut bowl with a tiny curved plane.

7. Takashi's aesthetic imprint can also be seen in his hand-tools: here, various kinds of plane.

8. Petal dishes in progress.

Tara Badcock

Australia

'If you can imagine holding a very old garment in your hand and peering down into the weave to find the most delicate mending stitches – a trace of love and attention to detail, and proof that someone valued that textile enough to preserve and repair it: this inspires me to translate my own artistic vision with a similar love and care,' says Tara Badcock. She dedicates herself to sourcing handmade antique textiles, mending them and altering them to allow a continuation of their history. 'Textiles are a social medium. Long before the internet was invented, human beings communicated through the "language" of their dress. Textiles are possibly the most powerful and sophisticated communicating tool we still have.' A native of Tasmania, Tara has another spiritual home in France. She lived in Paris for two years, 'renting a beautiful, light-filled apartment from a wonderful lady I worked for. One day I was making myself an embroidered and patched tea cosy for my favourite Limoges teapot, while listening to the quiet sounds of a weekend summer day, when I was hit by a wave of homesickness. All my memories of drinking tea with relatives, close friends and new acquaintances suddenly became poignant. I decided to create a project where I would make tea cosies as domestic

shrines to shared moments and personal histories.' Eventually the urge to move back to Australia grew too strong, though Tara plans to continue to visit France as an integral inspiration for her work. Conveying her love of all things theatrical (as a child, she dreamed of joining a circus or becoming a *comédienne* in a gilded Baroque theatre), her works are richly conceived. 'I love layering, collaging and printing onto fabrics before smothering the surface with tactile hand-embroidery – mainly in satin, feather, chain and buttonhole stitches – and sewing through thick layers to create contours and "body".' Tara's works often revel in opposites – heavy fabrics with lightweight, strong colours against delicate – and her love of languages may explain why she often embroiders texts. Her unique, flamboyant vision has brought her international recognition (collaborating on a suite at the Ice Hotel in Sweden; featuring in the art collections of the UNESCO headquarters in Paris and the Tasmanian Museum & Art Gallery in Hobart). This busy multitasker puts her heart and soul into everything she does.

See also p.315
www.tarabadcock.com

5

6

1, 2. Tara Badcock preparing a patchwork artwork.

3. Tribute to an Australian icon: a detail of the 'Empress' artwork, in hand- and freehand machine-embroidered silk.

4. A mantra for a spiritual pilgrimage: 'Desire', 'Seek' and 'Follow' cushions in embroidered silk, linen and hemp.

7

5. Tara hard at work on a dress.

6. The 'Arcadia Rosette', made of hand-embroidered silk. Tara particularly enjoys hand-stitching as it would have been done in pre-industrialization times.

7. A detail of the 'Scrimshaw' brooch, with embroidery on silk and linen, and wallaby bones.

Tara Shackell

Australia

Australian ceramicist Tara Shackell creates 'objects that are beautiful to use every day'. These are pieces that elevate whatever meal or flower they contain, the graceful, understated vessels honing earthy tones and serene volumes. 'I've been working with clay for some six years now. I'm still producing the white tableware that I developed while studying, but have also added quite diverse ranges of work. I hope that all of it conveys a sense of materiality, quietness and space, in different ways.' Tara's influences include Gwyn Hanssen Pigott, the Australian potter 'who made an art of arranging simple cups, bowls and bottles with subtlety' and Lucie Rie, 'whose wonderful glaze colours, sgraffito and footed bowls are instantly recognizable and still look contemporary'. In her own studio, Tara enjoys the meditative process of throwing pots on the wheel. 'I use glazes that respond to the colour or texture of the clay to create depth,' she notes. 'My white tableware is made from iron-rich clay and the colour comes through on the rims, where the glaze is thinner. I've also been using a lot of very strong cobalt blue on dark clays. I love the rich colour paired with the earth browns.' Tara originally graduated with a BA in fine art, majoring in photography. She later did a few evening classes in ceramics and loved it so much that she enrolled on a four-year part-time course at TAFE. 'I spent the whole week looking forward to the next class and I was always the last to pack up,' she smiles. 'The course included a strong design emphasis and a lot of skills training. I just wanted to be doing this *all* the time.' Her current studio is a tiny backyard bungalow, but with a huge south-facing window where Tara has placed her wheel. 'I like to have some finished work around me as references,' she says, 'and there are always pots in progress shuffled around.' Pottery is a notably slow process. 'To make a bowl, first it's thrown on the wheel. After a few days of drying, it's turned upside down and any excess clay is trimmed. Then there's another few days of drying before it goes into the kiln for a bisque firing. After that it's glazed, then it goes back into the kiln for final firing, which usually takes a day, with another day or two to cool down. The whole process might take six to eight weeks, then I make refinements and start again,' Tara explains. Her labour of love is much appreciated by all who see her works.

See also p.297
www.tarashackell.com

1. Glaze test tiles in a harmonious colour palette.

2. Tara Shackell enjoying life on the doorstep of her charming studio.

3. Pieces from the elegant, honest 'Rock' and 'Place' series in stoneware and porcelain.

4. The naked truth: thrown 'Rock' vases.

5. 'Dip' bowls in the process of being glazed.

230

9. Compact, bright and organized, yet full of personal touches: Tara's studio in Melbourne.

6. Tara shaping the base of a bowl.

7. Tools and stains, with which the magic happens.

8. Serene simplicity: a trio of 'Dip' bowls in thrown stoneware.

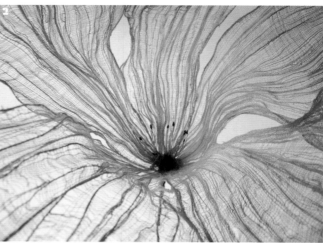

Ulrika Berge

Sweden

You could be forgiven for falling into a reverie when gazing at these giant botanical beauties. Suspended by nylon thread, they induce an overwhelming sense of serenity. 'I play with lines, creating drawings in the air,' explains their creator, Ulrika Berge. 'Thin lines have a fragility that is in some way emotional, and light gives shadow. My flowers float, dance or just spin slowly. They keep together or move apart. If you want to interact with them, you can. My love of threads and my wish to build pictures with threads is connected to my appreciation for organic beauty.' As a child, Ulrika wanted to be a carpenter and build furniture, but when she went to craft school she began to mix with artists and designers and realized that perhaps another path awaited. As she puts it: 'Becoming an artist was more or less an accident that worked out well.' She enrolled in the Bergen Academy of Art and Design in Norway, where she studied textiles for four and a half years. 'Although I rarely use it nowadays, weaving is perhaps the technique that affected me most. It's mathematical and magical, and has a strong symbolic value.' Over the years her work has evolved, ranging from huge, abstract installations to more figurative compositions. Once she began to experiment with shapes

and movement, 'suddenly there was a burst of flowers in my work...and they started to dance. I've continued to explore movement, also with my own body, through performance, animation and mechanical sculptures.' Ulrika is always full of ideas, 'but those that stay with me for a year or two are the ones that get a physical manifestation. My ideas are often a state of mind or a kind of tension that I want to explore. It's about finding the shape and colour combination that can embody these.' She often makes 3D sketches on paper and then starts to sew individual parts. 'I assemble these, sometimes finding new ways to use them. Then I sew more parts, and slowly a flower emerges. When the shape is complete, it's time for colour, using German reactive pigments. The final step is to test the movement.' It is no surprise that Ulrika's spellbinding artworks have been acquired by many institutions, such as town halls, hospitals and schools. One woman began to kiss the flowers, crying all the while. When she realized that Ulrika had made them, she turned to her and started kissing her instead. Her floral mobiles are a true balm for the soul.

See also p.250
www.ulrikaberge.se

1, 2. This detail of the 'Hypertrophy Mobile' somehow mirrors Ulrika Berge's flamboyant red mane!

3. Ulrika expertly sewing a new work.

4. Why not transform a plain wall into a ravishing field in summertime? The 'Nature Morte – Drawing in the Air' is made of sewn thread.

5. Simply ethereal: an 'Adventive Plant' sculpture in mixed media.

6

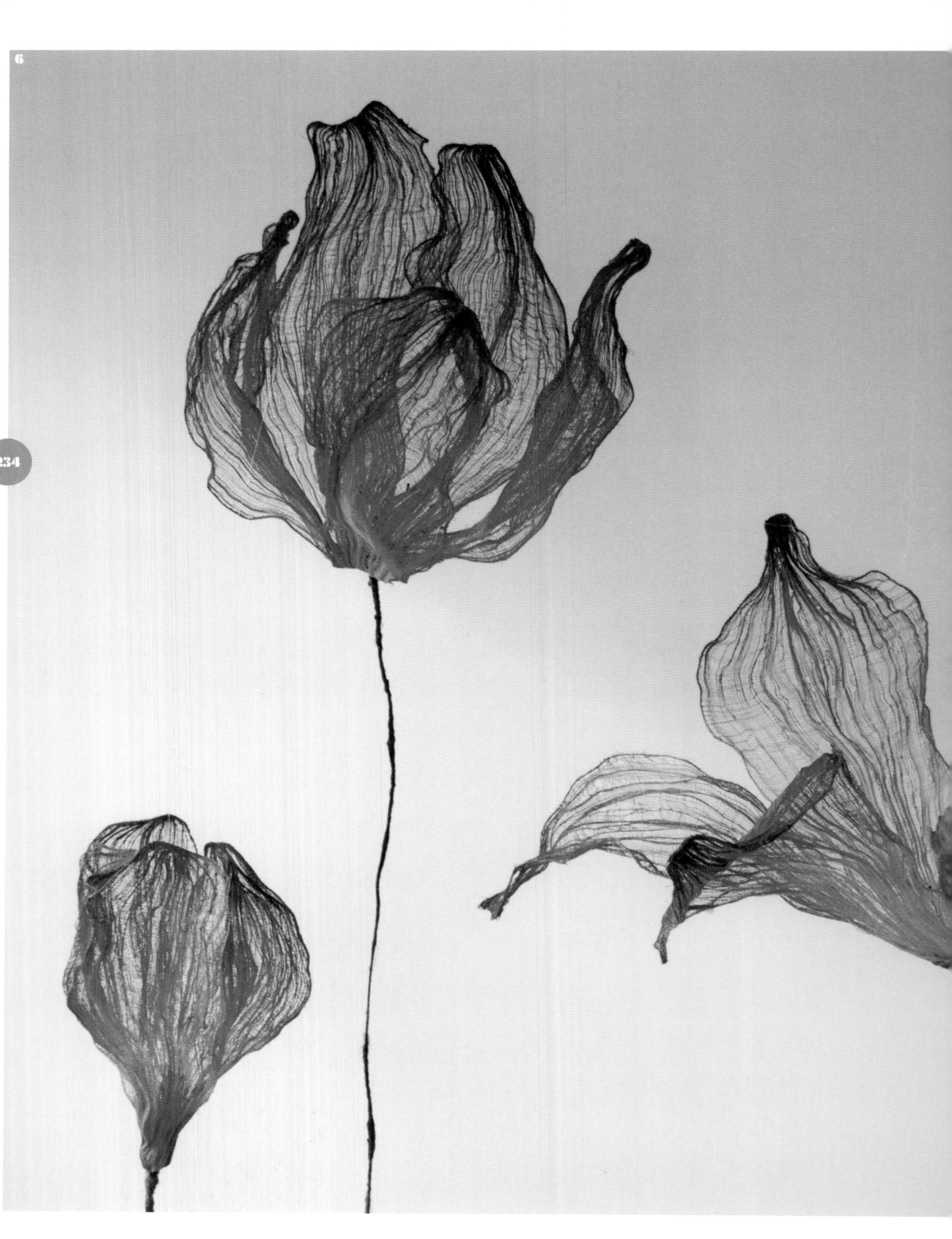

6. Rocking in the air, as if to the tune of an inaudible lullaby, the 'Hypertrophy Mobile' in mixed media.

7. Ulrika adjusting an 'Adventive Plant' sculpture (or perhaps she is gathering pollen?).

8. There is always a master plan behind the apparently random way a piece is stitched together.

Vanilla Bicycles

USA

Many people will recall their first attempts at riding a bicycle: a true rite of passage. Now think about custom-made bikes and the extra advantages they might confer. Self-described 'obsessive-compulsive' Sacha White of Vanilla Bicycles will build a bike to meet your every need. 'It's easy for handmade bikes to be pigeonholed as a luxury, but that's because we need to talk more about the deeper value they can bring,' says Sacha. 'When you have fit, fabrication and design all under one roof, you get a ride that can't be found in a mass-produced bike.' This representative of the 'skate/snowboard and hip-hop generation' started out by messengering, racing and tricking out friends' bikes, but, just as he was feeling that something was missing, he broke his own bicycle and someone suggested that he take it to a 'frame builder' for repair. 'I'd never heard of a frame builder before and had never thought about where bike frames came from, let alone different methods of construction. When I showed up at Tim Paterek's house, he was in the middle of brazing a new frame together. What I saw seemed like alchemy. This was the "something more" I was looking for.' Sacha has now been working with steel for over fifteen years. In that time, he has learned much about resources

and processes, including machining, getting parts cast and laser-cut, working in CAD for design and laying down graphics with paint rather than decals. He also works directly with manufacturers to have parts made to his own specifications. 'This helps me get closer to making things exactly the way I want them, rather than relying on stock pieces from a distributor.' Customers now visit Sacha from all over the world. 'I most enjoy nailing the design so that it fits the rider better than they've ever had it before and rides like it should: if it's a road bike, it should ride like a great road bike, a touring bike should ride like a great touring bike, etc. One of my jobs is to make a bike that's going to inspire its owner to ride.' Sacha particularly enjoys making bikes as gifts for loved ones. Case in point: the mould–breaking tricycle he took two and a half months to make for his younger daughter, Delilah. 'It was like the kid in me that always wanted to create finally could, because the adult in me had the skills! What the world needs is more works that are uncompromised and heartfelt; works that meet "the pursuit of excellence".' A philosophical ride we will gladly take…

See also p.290
www.vanillabicycles.com

1. Sacha White pondering at his workbench in Portland, Oregon.

2. 'V' for Vanilla Bicycles, a made-to-measure signature emblem.

3. A 'Cruiser' bicycle in elegant khaki green with leather fittings. What a cool way to commute!

4. Brazing seat stays to dropouts on a 'Speedvagen' commission.

5. With an eagle eye, Sacha calibrates seat stays to the seat tube.

6. Ready for all weather conditions: a '2012 Vanilla Single Speed Cross Racer'.

7. A trip back to childhood as you've never quite seen it: the award-winning 'Vanilla Tricycle', originally created for daughter Delilah.

8. Precision and an eye for detail: fitting 'Speedvagen' seat stays to the seat tube.

Young-I Kim

Germany

'The best compliment I have ever received is when my professor and mentor told me I could now call him by his first name and that we were at the same level of expertise,' beams Young-I Kim. Born and raised in Korea, she studied interior design at the Hansei University in Kunpo. While there, her professor told her that she would fit in well in Germany. 'So I watched a TV documentary and got hooked on the country,' she notes. With the support of her father, she moved to Bonn to learn the language and then began to search for a suitable university. She ended up studying metal design at the University of Applied Sciences and Arts in Hildesheim, where she still lives today, operating out of a workshop shared with a potter and a goldsmith. Her signature range is the deceptively simple 'Characterized Vessels' series. Exercises in abstract portraiture, each vessel represents one of Young-I's loved ones. 'Looking at and listening to someone dear to me, I imagine what colour and shape he or she would be,' she explains. 'The vessels show my idea of a person, and I believe viewers can get the same feeling.' On close examination, each reveals unique idiosyncrasies: a gentle bend to the left, a change in proportion, a variation in the application of gold leaf. The selection of colours is the pivotal step that cements the DNA. 'Selecting colours is my favourite part of the creative process,' says Young-I. 'I also thoroughly enjoy the making. Each vessel is executed in copper and raised by hand. The sides are enamelled with opaque enamel powder and this is applied in many layers, fired repeatedly and then ground by hand, polished and finished with a layer of wax.' Finally, the insides are plated with gold leaf, like light shining out of a delicate crater. Many clients report that they feel a sense of fulfilment and relaxation when they look upon Young-I's work. Unsurprisingly, she has won multiple prizes, including the Sponsorship award for creative handicraft at Handwerksform, the Talente award at Handwerkskammer, the Justus Brinckmann sponsorship award, the WCC-Europe EUNIQUE Award for Contemporary Crafts, the Three Lions Club Hanau Prize, the Grassi award and Silver prize at the 'Pushing Boundaries & Chasing Challenges' international metal art show in Beijing. 'Evolution comes from repetition and experience,' Young-I emphasizes. Her works, rendering pure emotion and conveying humanity, are nothing short of genius.

See also p.288
See also p.288
www.youngikim.de

1, 5. Young-I Kim planishing the surface of a bowl.

2, 9. The essential tools of a silversmith.

3. A 'Characterized Vessel' in copper, enamel and gold leaf, made with processes including hand-raising, planishing, enamelling and gold leaf plating.

4. An alchemist's vials: dozens of bottles containing enamel colour pigments.

6. Hand-raising a vessel.

7. Sprinkling enamel powder.

8. Heating the enamel by placing the vessel in the kiln.

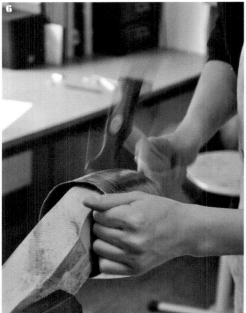

10

11

8

9

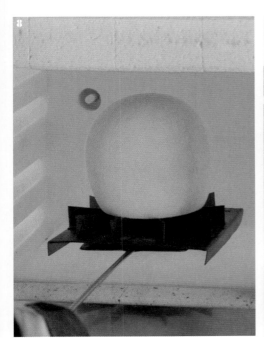

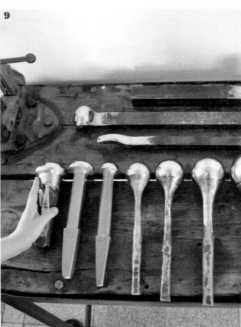

10–13. A multicoloured line-up, each opening bearing slightly serrated edges like cut-open eggshells: 'Characterized Vessels' in copper and enamel with gold leaf plating.

243

12

13

Zoé Ouvrier

France

Step into a forest whose stark beauty exudes Asian zen and European elegance…from the comfort of your own home. Zoé Ouvrier's meticulously engraved pieces function as much as works of art (wall panels) as they do as useful furnishings (folding screens). They all showcase breathtaking nature-inspired patterns – tree trunks, foliage, branches and rhizomes. 'A Chinese friend introduced me to woodcarving when I was still a student at the Beaux-Arts school in Paris. I very quickly felt comfortable with it, and it's been in my life for fifteen years,' Zoe explains. 'Recently I've also found out that I'm dyslexic. It's been such a burden, as I've always been a bit socially awkward. No wonder the relaxing, rather solitary aspect of woodcarving appealed to me.' Zoé had to fend for herself very early, and at one point dabbled in modelling, but her heart had long been in art. 'I've always drawn with felt pen in notebooks. My drawings caught the eye of some kindly mentors, and, thanks to those great encounters, I grew more confident,' she says. During her Beaux-Arts years, she mastered the art of moulding, a technique that in turn fine-tuned her approach towards 3D objects. Now she sculpts and paints plywood panels with virtuosic ability, carving flat surfaces into bark, a chip at a time.

The choice of plywood is key to her broader artistic statement: wood that has been processed by humans is now metaphorically returned to its organic state. 'Through my works I am questioning where we come from versus where we go. It's about the importance of "imprint"; what we leave behind.' Interior designers, architects and private clients have been drawn to her work, and examples can be found in top hotels, offices and homes. Admirers respect the time-consuming nature of the work, and the scale of most of Zoé's pieces makes this a particular factor: a 230 x 200 cm (90½ x 78¾ in.) screen can take up to six weeks to complete. The painstaking process involves the transfer of an initial sketch onto a large surface, though Zoé also embraces the unexpected. 'I respect chance outcomes and the inevitability of errors,' she says. Long walks looking for seeds counterbalance the hours of hermit-like absorption in her workshop. 'I suspect that my urban environment may influence my work, so I try to shield myself from it as much as possible.' Her remarkable botanical replicas are the perfect screen.

See also p.265
www.zoeouvrier.com

1. Sculpting on a flat surface: Zoé Ouvrier meticulously hand-carves individual elements of bark.

2. Zoé standing in front of a forest of her own making: the 'White' screen in wood and acrylic paint.

3. Zoé painting an outline prior to chiselling. Her works sit somewhere between painting and sculpture: *peintures objets*, as she calls them.

4. Cold chisels and gouges are the tools of her trade.

5. A 'Knot Panel' engraved sculpture, made of wood with acrylic paint.

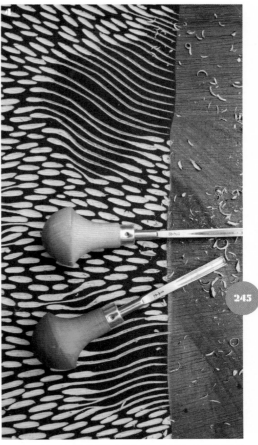

245

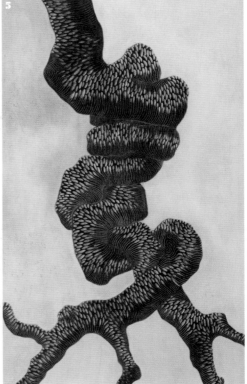

6. 'India' screen: engraved sculpture in wood and acrylic paint.

7. 'Liloo' screen: engraved sculpture in wood and acrylic paint.

Art

Maïssa Toulet

1. 'Sans Fin Brassé et Trituré': seashells, coral and recycled plaster mould.

2. 'Autoportrait': porcelain doll and taxidermied wild boar foot.

3. 'Cimetière Marin': seashells, coral, recycled plaster mould and cut-out pictures.

1

2

3

Susan Hipgrave

4. 'Circus Cyaneus – Hen Harrier', earthenware and black ink.

5. 'Cereus Berlandieri', earthenware and black ink.

6. 'Caltha Palustri Flore Simplici', earthenware and black ink.

7. 'Cephalotus Follicularis', earthenware and black ink.

8. 'Aesculus Hippocastanum', earthenware and black ink.

5

6

7

8

250

Ulrika Berge

1, 3. 'Blue Mobile', mixed media.

2. 'To Let Go' moving sculpture (detail), mixed media.

4

5

Domenica More Gordon

4–6. 'Show Dogs', felt and textile, made for an Arts & Science exhibition in Tokyo.

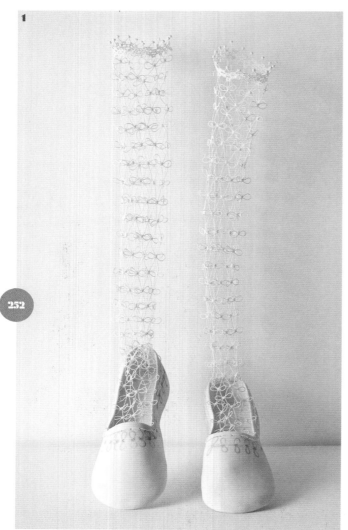

Aude Tahon

1. 'Les Chaussons de Madame De': porcelain (*mishima*) shoes with silk thread (Korean knots technique) gaiters.

2. 'Paire de Souliers': porcelain (*mishima*) shoes with cotton/polyester braid (Korean knots technique) socks.

Emmanuelle Dupont

3. 'Jeunes Pousses Elytrée', mixed media and techniques.

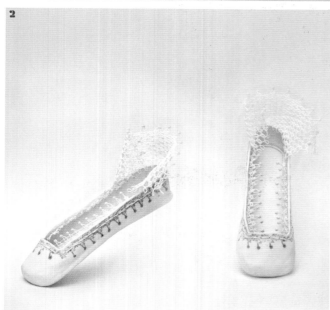

2

253

Michaël Cailloux

4. 'Mantis Reugiosa': etching, aquatint and copper, 'Insectes' series, 'Mouches' collection.

5. 'Cycloptera Speculata': etching, aquatint and copper, 'Insectes' series, 'Mouches' collection.

6. 'Nature Morte': etching, aquatint and copper, 'Natures Mortes' series, 'Mouches' collection.

7. 'Anax Imperator': etching, aquatint and copper, 'Insectes' series, 'Mouches' collection.

Ceramics

Lise Meunier

1. 'Couronne et Bouquet': enamelled faïence flowers, antique fabrics and glass domes.

2. 'Nature Morte': enamelled faïence flowers, blue fabric and glass dome.

3

4

5

6

7

Suna Fujita

3. 'Cake Shop' pot with lid (*futamono*): wheel-thrown pottery, painting with coloured slip and overglaze.

4. 'Jaguar and Jungle Pattern' *futamono*: wheel-thrown pottery, painting with coloured slip and overglaze.

5. 'Penguin' candy pot (*furidashi*): wheel-thrown pottery, painting with coloured slip and overglaze.

6. 'Sea Bathing' teapot (*potto*): wheel-thrown pottery, painting with coloured slip and overglaze.

7. 'Bathhouse' *potto* (detail): wheel-thrown pottery, painting with coloured slip and overglaze.

Amy Jayne Hughes

1. 'Winged Porcelain' urn and plinth.

2. 'Handbuilt Stoneware' vases, from the 'Trésor Découvert' series.

Katharine Morling

3. 'Inside Out': earthstone, porcelain slip, black stain and blown mirrored glass.

4. 'Two-Headed Fish and Seahorse': earthstone, porcelain, porcelain slip and black stain, from the 'Morling and the Hoard' series.

5. 'Cut': earthstone, porcelain slip and black stain.

6. 'Vase of Stems': porcelain and black stain.

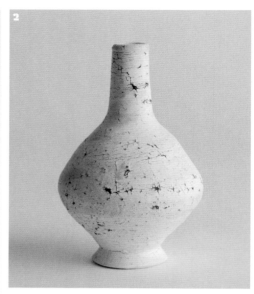

Matthias Kaiser

1. 'Holy Water' vase, stoneware.

2. 'Cracked Slip' vase, stoneware.

3. 'Brancusi Pillar-Style' wall vase, porcelain.

4. 'Copper' vase, stoneware.

5. 'Jar', stoneware.

6

Clémentine Dupré

6. 'Architecture #10': stoneware, engobe and enamel, 'Architectonique' series.

7. 'Axiomatique #5': stoneware and enamel, 'Axiomatique' series.

8. 'Architecture #3': stoneware, engobe and enamel, 'Architectonique' series.

7

8

Furniture

Sebastian Cox

1. 'Suent Superlight' chairs (clockwise from bottom left: black, pink, white, grey) in coppiced timber, from the 'Silviculture' series.

1

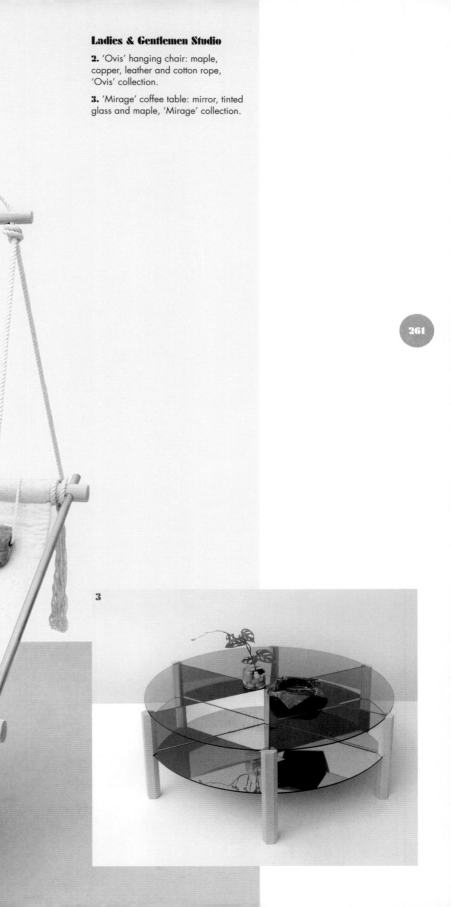

Ladies & Gentlemen Studio

2. 'Ovis' hanging chair: maple, copper, leather and cotton rope, 'Ovis' collection.

3. 'Mirage' coffee table: mirror, tinted glass and maple, 'Mirage' collection.

3

1

2

3

Res Anima

1. 'Bankl' two- or three-seater in ash, 'Seating Furniture' collection.

2. 'Tavola' table in smoked oak and cast bronze.

3. 'Hockl' three-legged stool with chair elements, in ash, 'Seating Furniture' collection.

5

Oferenda Objetos

4, 5. 'Fractal' armchair: crocheted polyester rope, wood and foam seat, stainless steel frame, 'Fractal' collection.

6. 'Jangada' balance chair: polyester rope and aluminium, 'Jangada' collection.

7. 'Jangada' seat: polyester rope and aluminium, 'Jangada' collection.

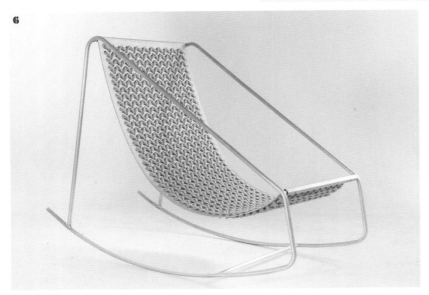

Greg Hatton

1. 'Denim' bean bag in denim fabric.

2. 'Kids' bed in reclaimed Oregon (Douglas fir wood), with building block details.

3. 'Lab Bar' stool in Victorian ash, with black steel legs.

4. 'Hairpin Leg' stool in ironbark, with green steel legs.

5. 'Milk Made' stool, a rounded three-legged stool in ironbark and sugar gum.

Zoé Ouvrier

6. 'Noa' screen (front): engraved sculpture, oil and acrylic paint, 'Forest' collection.

7. 'Paula' screen (front): engraved sculpture, acrylic paint, 'Forest' collection.

8. 'Sensible': engraved sculpture, oil paint, 'Lace' collection.

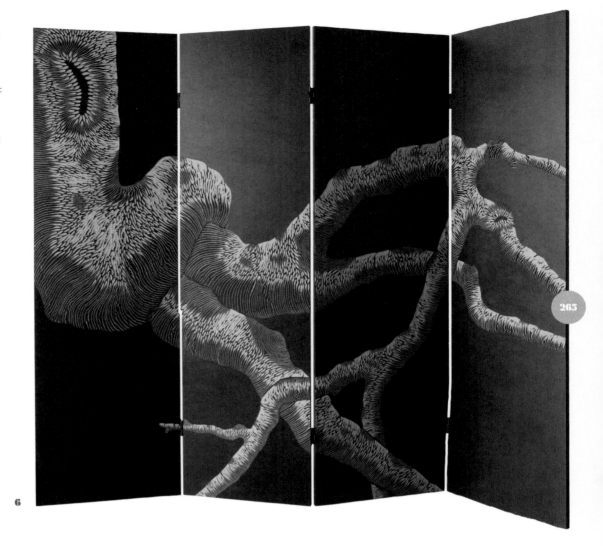

6

265

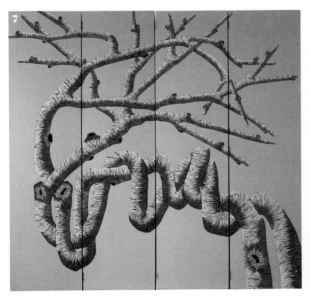

7

8

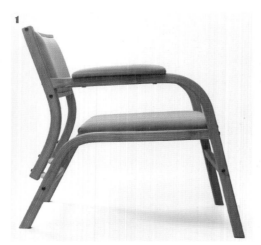

1

2

Brothers Dressler

1. 'Elbow "Ollie"' lounge and work chair: ash, 'Out of Quarantine' series.

2. 'Mesh' screen: walnut, maple, pine, poplar, cherry, mahogany, cedar and elm, 'Cut Ups' series.

Savo&Pomelina

3. 'Closet Television': beech, plywood, print and wool, 'Ton' collection.

4. 'Tabouret': beech and wool, 'Ton' collection.

5. 'Roller Table': beech, linoleum and cotton, 'Acrobat' collection.

3

4

5

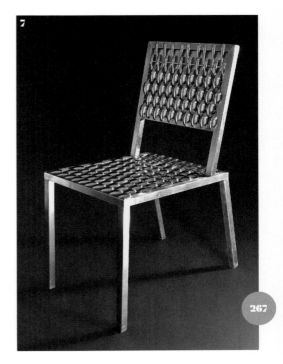

Leo Capote

6. 'Egg Porcas' armchair: carbon steel nuts and Electroless nickel.

7. 'Cohler' chair: stainless steel frame and spoons.

8. 'Martelo' table: nine hammers, PU varnish and glass top.

9. 'Chairs 18': eighteen hammers, carbon steel plate and PU varnish.

Glasswork

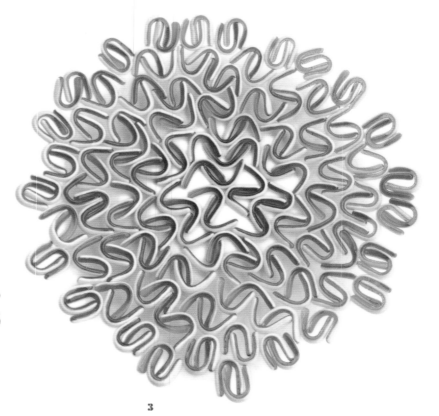

Manuela Castro Martins

1. 'Glass Lace II' black and crystal plate.

2. 'Glass Lace I' purple and silver plate.

3. 'Glass Lace II' amber and ivory plate.

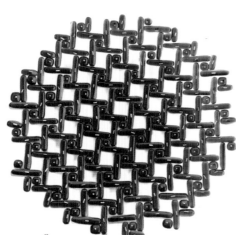

2

3

Hanne Enemark

4. 'Fondue' vessels: blown glass dipped in molten glass with 22ct gold, 'Fondue' series.

5. 'Cristal' vessel: soft blown glass with yellow and lime glass stones, 'Cristal' series.

6. 'Fool's Gold' vessel: soft blown glass with gold-covered solid glass cubes, 'Fool's Gold' series.

Nyholm Cantrell

1. 'Blast Off' sculpture by Ned Cantrell: blown and hot-sculpted glass with steel.

2. Decanters by Karen Nyholm: blown glass.

3. 'Tiger' double bowl by Karen Nyholm: blown glass, sandblasting, porcelain figurine and stainless steel, 'Double Bowls' series.

4. 'Reticello Fries' by Ned Cantrell: blown glass.

1

Bee Kingdom

5. 'Solar Temple' sculpture by Ryan Marsh Fairweather: blown and sandblasted glass.

6. 'Electrophauns' sculptures by Ryan Marsh Fairweather: blown and sandblasted glass.

7. 'Mythopoet' sculpture: blown glass, collaborative series.

272

1

2

3

4

5

6

7

273

8

Bethamy Linton

1. 'Hairpin': hand-cut anodized titanium, embossed silver and silver pins, 'Swallowfish' series.

2. 'Lucky' necklace in embossed sterling silver.

3. 'Fade' ring: hand-cut anodized titanium and sterling silver, 'Bloom' series.

4. Earrings in embossed sterling silver, 'Pepper' series.

5. 'Fuss' hairpin in hand-cut anodized titanium (back) and embossed sterling silver.

Anne Léger

6. 'Nude' necklace: wood, silver cast, silver, copper, enamel and stone.

7. 'Carnation' necklace: wood, silver, copper, enamel and stone.

8. 'Plastron' necklace: wood, silver and stones.

Ana Hagopian

1. 'Raspberry' necklace, mixed techniques.

2. 'Round', 'Sponge' and 'Arc' bracelets, mixed techniques.

3

Renata Meirelles

3. 'CIZ' neckpiece, silk cord and taffeta, 'Score Family' collection.

4. 'CIR 5X' shawl, taffeta, 'CIR Family' collection.

5. 'REN 115' neckpiece, taffeta, 'REN Family' collection.

4

5

Jevda

1. 'Sous le Ciel Ensoleillé' neck ornament: vintage Indian silk sari, embroidered Uzbek panel, French rosary beads and mother-of-pearl buttons, with coloured wooden beads and tassels.

2. 'La Déesse aux Eléphants' opera coat and 'Ma Robe à Moi' dress: vintage silk saris.

3. (left) 'Les Oiseaux du Paradis' stole: Indian saris with appliqués of embroidered Uzbek birds of happiness and flowers; (right) 'Palazzo Orfei' opera coat: patchwork of embroidered saris, worn with 'Les Chapelets de Tante Sido' necklaces made with vintage French wooden rosary beads.

276

Aude Tahon

4. Black headpiece: polyester/cotton braiding (Korean knots technique), coated paper sheath.

5. 'Flocon' headpiece: polyester/cotton braiding (Korean knots technique), silk particles.

6. White collar: polyester/cotton braiding (Korean knots technique).

7. Fingerless glove: polyester/cotton braiding (Korean knots technique).

277

Iida-Kasaten

1. 'Vegetable Sticks' umbrella in printed polyester and wood.

2. 'Pressed Flowers' umbrella in printed polyester and wood.

Margit Seland

3, 4. 'Phases' vases for yourself or the wall: cast coloured porcelain, various glazes and ribbons.

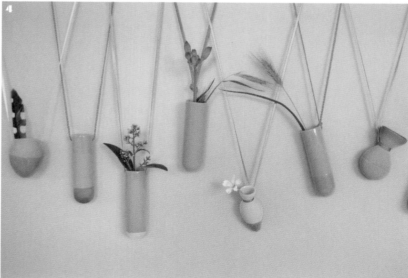

5

6

7

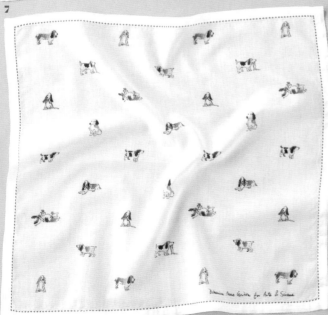

8

Content & Container

1. 'Parcelbag 3' in hand-printed leather (screen-print), 'Parcelbag' collection.

2. 'Parcelbag 1' in hand-printed leather (screen-print), 'Parcelbag' collection.

Maxime Leroy

3. 'Sacco Baret No. 3' prototype black sneakers: leather and black goose coquille (breast) feathers.

4. 'Colibri' brooch: handmade skull in resin with iron oxide, and swallow-tailed hummingbird feathers.

Michaël Cailloux

5. 'Offrande' scarf in grey, printed silk.

6. 'Poissons' scarf in absinthe, printed silk.

7. 'Peigne' scarf in white and blue, printed silk.

281

Lighting

1

2

3

Brothers Dressler

1. 'Branches' chandelier: responsibly sourced hardwood, E12 candelabra sockets and machine hardware, 'Branches' series.

2. 'Hoop Light III': off-cuts from the making of chaise longue, simple bed and shelving systems, combined with obsolete bicycle rims and spokes, a cold cathode compact fluorescent bulb and an acrylic diffuser, 'Cut Ups' collection.

Ladies & Gentlemen Studio

3. 'Maru' pendant lights in glass, brass or copper tubing, paperstone and wood, 'Maru' collection.

Leo Capote

4. 'Ferro Ouro Rose' lamp: 1960s iron (base), flexible LED lamp, rose gold finish.

5. 'Bigorna Ouro' lamp: steel anvil (base), steel bathroom rods, gold finish.

283

1

5

Papier à Êtres

1. 'Mademoiselle Plume' lamp, papier-mâché, metal frame.

2. 'Anatole' wall lamp, papier-mâché, metal frame.

3. 'Amandine' wall lamp, papier-mâché, metal frame.

4. 'Muguet' wall lamp, papier-mâché, metal frame.

2

3

4

Sebastian Cox

5. 'Rod' desk lamp in coppiced timber.

Hanne Enemark

6. 'Phototaxis' lights in blown and
cast glass, 'Photoaxis' series.

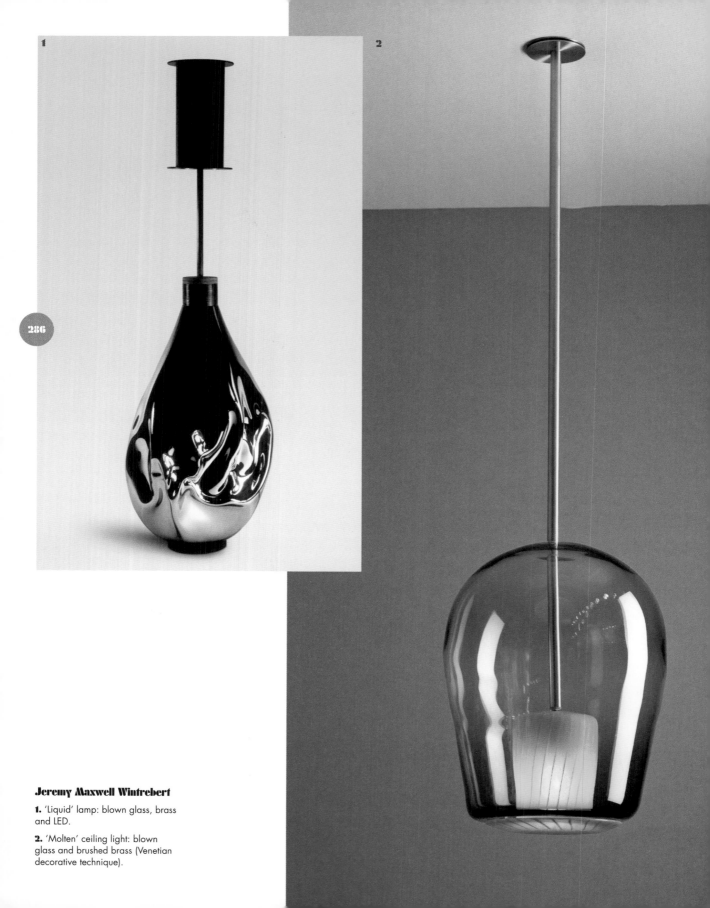

Jeremy Maxwell Wintrebert

1. 'Liquid' lamp: blown glass, brass and LED.

2. 'Molten' ceiling light: blown glass and brushed brass (Venetian decorative technique).

Naomi Paul

3. 'Glück' ceiling light in dark navy/ mustard yellow: hand-crocheted 1- and 2-ply mercerized cotton cord, seamless finish, powder-coated framework.

4. 'Glück' ceiling light in white/ ember: hand-crocheted 1- and 2-ply mercerized cotton cord, seamless finish, powder-coated framework.

5. 'Glück' ceiling light in ember: hand-crocheted 1- and 2-ply mercerized cotton cord, seamless finish, powder-coated framework.

6. 'Sonne' ceiling light in mustard yellow/dark navy: hand-crocheted 2-ply mercerized cotton cord (double cloth), seamless finish, powder-coated framework.

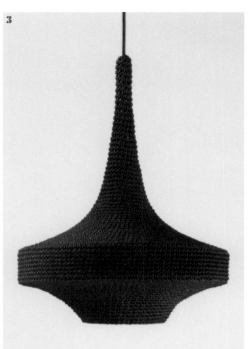

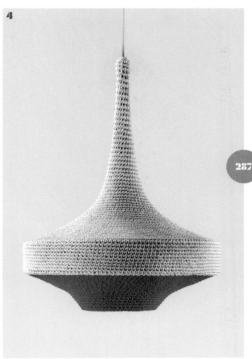

287

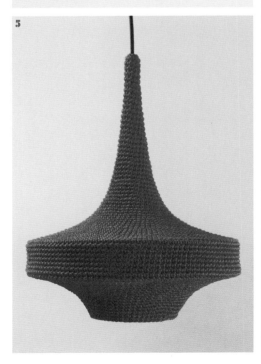

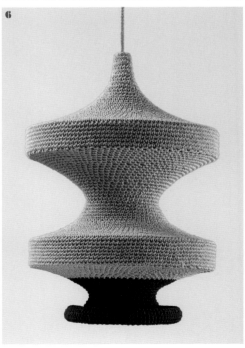

Metalwork

Young-I Kim

1–5. 'Characterized Vessels' in copper, enamel and gold leaf.

1

2

3

4

5

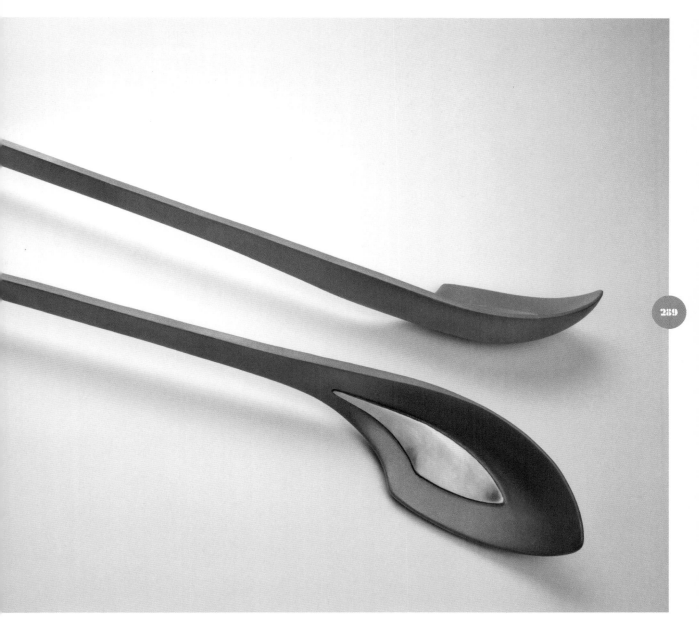

Bethany Linton

6. A set of door handles (1 of 20), commissioned by St George's Cathedral, Perth: masters cast in wood, then in white brass with red bronze inlay.

7. 'King Brown' box in hand-cut anodized titanium and sterling silver.

Vanilla Bicycles

1. '2012 Speedvagen Surprise Me!
Cross Machine'.

2, 4. '2013 Speedvagen White
Hollow Text Road Machine'.

3. '2014 Speedvagen Horizon
Road Machine'.

Cathy Miles

5. 'Stone Curlew' sculpture: wire, found materials, 'Common Bird Life' series.

6. 'Cockatiel' sculpture: wire, found materials, 'Common Bird Life' series.

7. 'Neil's Shoes' (detail): collection of five sculptures in wire.

5

6

291

7

Papercraft

Michaël Cailloux

1. 'Insectes' wallpaper.

Jude Miller

2. 'Nasturtium' for the hair, crepe paper.

3. 'American Selection with Blue Spiderwort', crepe paper, 'Americas' collection.

4. 'Roses and Blackberries' for the hair, crepe paper.

5. 'White Bryony' for the hair, crepe paper and beads.

Paper-Cut-Project

5, 7. 'Seahorse Crown' (front and side): paper, exclusive collection for La Mer.

6. 'Driftwood Crown' (front): paper, exclusive collection for La Mer.

8. 'Octopus Crown' (side): paper, exclusive collection for La Mer.

Jennifer Collier

1. 'Telephone' sculpture: vintage telephone directories, grey board and machine stitch.

2. 'Binoculars' sculpture: vintage sheet music, grey board and machine stitch.

3. 'Singer Sewing Machine' sculpture: vintage dressmaking patterns and instructions, grey board and machine stitch.

4. 'Paper Watering Can' sculpture: vintage nursery storybook pages, grey board and machine stitch.

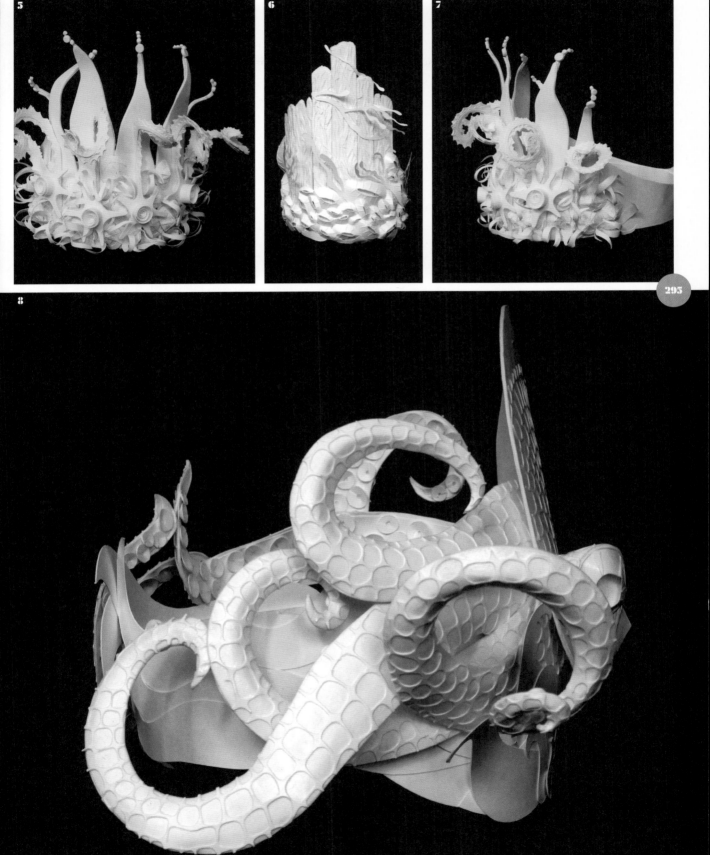

Tableware

Ben Fiess

1. Container in porcelain and stoneware.

2. Bottle in porcelain and stoneware.

3. Vase in porcelain and stoneware.

1

2

3

Clémentine Dupré

4. 'Micro-organisme' limited edition series in porcelain, with porcelain pearls and enamel.

4

5

Tara Shackell

5. 'Topography' series: stoneware, thrown and inlaid with oxides.

6. 'White Tableware 3': thrown stoneware, 'White Tableware' series.

7. 'Rock' collection: stoneware, thrown and hand-built, 'Rock' series.

6

7

Diana Fayt

1. 'Rabbits Speak a Secret Language' square platter: hand-built stoneware, underglazes, stains and glaze.

2. 'Canteen' vase: stoneware, slipcast, underglazes, stains and glaze.

3. Handmade bowls: stoneware, slipcast, underglazes, stains and glaze.

4. Handmade tumblers: stoneware, slipcast, underglazes, stains and glaze.

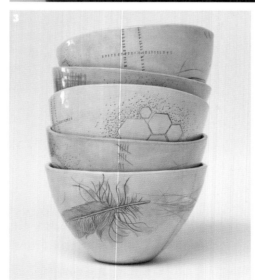

Margit Seland

5. 'Salt-stone' dishes in hand-formed porcelain and stoneware.

6. 'Tide' jugs and cups in cast, coloured porcelain.

7. 'Pinched Pitcher' jugs in cast, coloured porcelain.

8. 'Sugar-bag' in cast porcelain.

9. 'Scoop' cups and bowls in cast, coloured porcelain.

299

Takashi Tomii

1. Fork and knife in birch, finished with natural oil.

2. Series of 'Shikimono' trays in oak, finished with natural oil.

3. Round tray in chestnut, dyed and polished with rice bran.

4. Soup spoons in cherry, finished with natural oil.

Matthias Kaiser

5. 'Platinum Vases with Sand Base' in stoneware.

6. 'Assembled' pitcher in porcelain.

7. 'Onggi Bauhaus' teapot in stoneware with iron handle.

8. 'Bauhaus Kyusu' teapot in porcelain with wooden handle.

9. 'Black Turtle' vase in stoneware.

6

7

8

9

5

Claydies

1, 2. 'Snout' cups in cast porcelain with gold logo, 'This is not a joke' collection.

3. 'True Feelings' tableware collection in hand-modelled porcelain with transparent glaze.

Content & Container

4. 'C-Set' mix-and-match coffee sets in porcelain.

5. 'Traces' collection: hand-cut wood, moulded and poured into black porcelain.

6. 'Woodraw' vessels collection: chainsaw-cut wood, moulded and poured into porcelain.

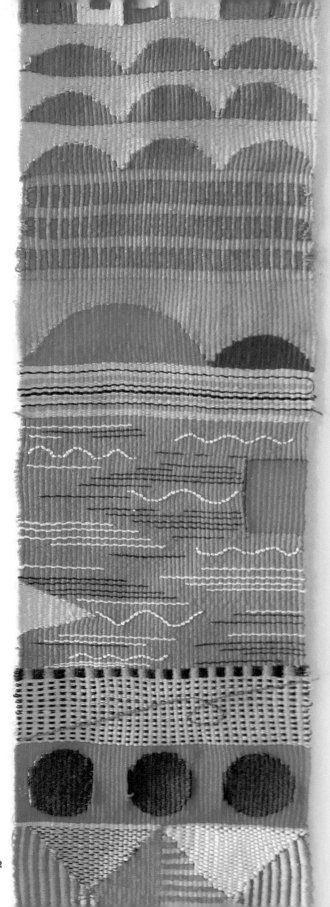

Textiles & Homewares

Decorative

1

2

Hannah Waldron

1. 'Kurukuru' tapestry, various yarns, for Landfill Editions.

2. 'Kreuzberg' tapestry (detail), various yarns, 'The Map Tapestries' series.

3. 'Maze' weaving, various yarns, private collection.

Sally Nencini

4. 'Shoe' stool: mid-century G-Plan stool, upholstery and stitchwork by Sally Nencini, design by Peter Nencini.

5. 'Pea and Poppy' stool: upholstery and embroidery by Sally Nencini, design by Peter Nencini.

6. 'Tyrella' chair (detail): upholstery and embroidery by Sally Nencini, design by Peter Nencini.

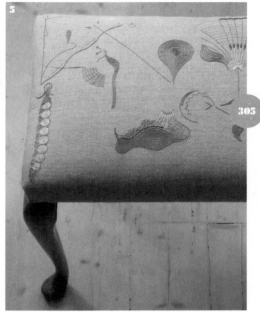

305

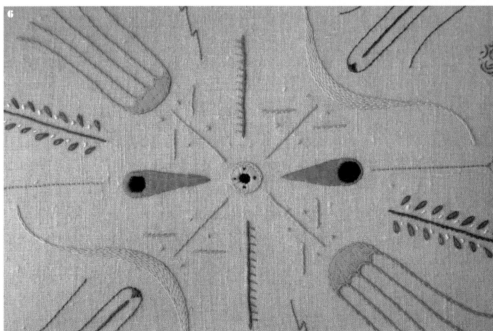

Mister Finch

1. 'Sleeping Fox with Cape' sculpture, vintage textiles.

2. 'Flower Moth' pair, vintage seat cover and fake fur.

3. 'Butterflies', vintage tablecloths.

Rosemary Milner

4. 'Woodlark' (detail), etching and embroidery from original artwork onto found vintage fabric, 'Willow Bank' collection.

5. 'Tree Sparrow', etching and embroidery from original artwork onto found vintage doily, 'Willow Bank' collection.

5

Abigail Brown

1. 'Golden Oriole', fabric.
2. 'Green Woodpecker', fabric.
3. 'Blue Winged Pitta', fabric.
4. 'Peacock', fabric.
5. 'American Flamingo', fabric.

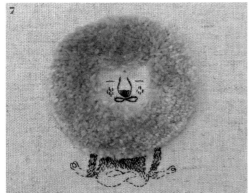

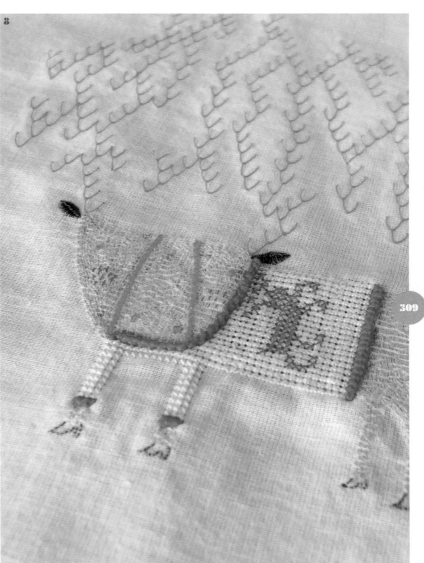

309

Miga de Pan

6. 'Lion Mask' embroidery.

7. 'Lion Buddha' embroidery.

8. 'Deer with Sweater with Deer Detail' embroidery.

9. 'But I Didn't Want' embroidery.

Textiles & Homewares
Functional

Karen Barbé

1. Handwoven cushion: 8-shaft table loom, merino wool and angora hair.

2. Screen-printed apron: cotton twill, 'Copihue' collection.

3. Potholders: needlepoint stitch, wool and organic cotton sateen for backing.

310

1

2

3

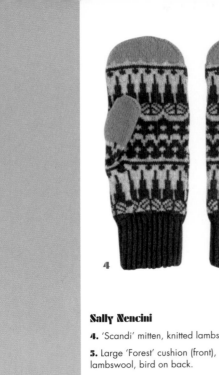

Sally Nencini

4. 'Scandi' mitten, knitted lambswool.

5. Large 'Forest' cushion (front), lambswool, bird on back.

6. Large 'Cat and Mouse' cushion (front), lambswool, mouse on back.

7. 'Dapper Dog', knitted lambswool, hand-embroidered face with wool felt eyes.

8. Small 'Tulips and Daisies' cushion, lambswool.

4

5

6

7

8

1

2

Polly Burton

1. 'Starfish' cushion, screen-print on hemp.

2. 'Seaweed' cushion, screen-print on linen.

Catarina Riccabona

3. Handwoven linen cushion with red stripes.

4. Handwoven linen cushion with white stripes.

4

3

5. 'Maru' hand mirror in brass or copper with Corian, 'Maru' collection.

6. 'Cylinder' salt and pepper shakers in copper.

7. 'Perimeter' tray in white oak or walnut, with brass, powder-coated aluminium, Carrera marble and rubber (tray shown here with 'Cylinder' shakers in brass).

6

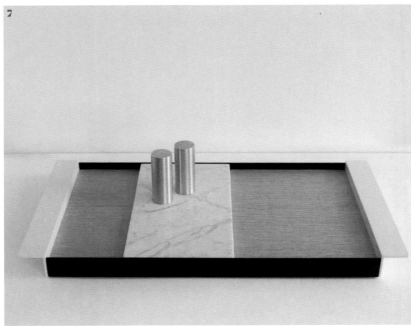

7

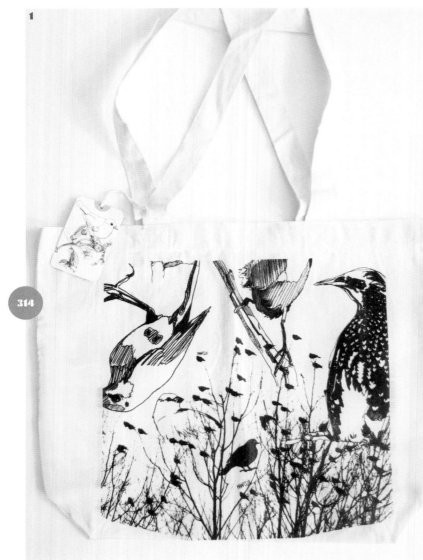

Maartje van den Noort

1. Ecru tote bag, eco cotton with silkscreen print.

2. Black tote bag, eco cotton with silkscreen print in gold.

3, 4. 'Starling' cushions, eco linen with silkscreen.

5   6   7

8

Savo&Pomelina

5. 'Pomegranate' cushion, print on cotton, 'Fudge' collection.

6. 'Rosa' cushion, embroidery on wool, 'Tikka' collection.

7. 'Scarabée' cushion, embroidery on wool, 'Tikka' collection.

Tara Badcock

8. 'Colonial Letter' cushion, hand- and freehand machine-embroidered silk and linen, 'Postal Fictions' collection.

9. 'Stag Beetle' cushion, hand- and freehand machine-embroidered silk, private commission.

10. 'Encyclopaedia Tasmanicus' giant dice, 6 of 13 appliquéd and stitched leather cubes: collection for Little Penguins Bicheno childcare centres.

9

10

Resources

Recommended shops

The unique, the whimsical, the desirable, the exceptional… These addresses are among my favourite places to visit, be it to shop, to indulge, to treat someone or simply to recharge my mind with creative and inspirational sights. The list is highly subjective and non-exhaustive.

London
DARKROOM
52 Lamb's Conduit Street, WC1N 3LL
Tel +44 (0)20 7831 7244
www.darkroomlondon.com
The place to go for contemporary, stylish independent designers' creations.

Gallery Eclectic
66 Marylebone High Street, W1U 5JF
http://eclectic66.co.uk
Japanese arts and crafts in the heart of London.

J&B The Shop
158a Columbia Road, E2 7RG
http://jessieandbuddugtheshop.blogspot.com
Two passionate makers' wonderland.

Luna & Curious
24–26 Calvert Avenue, E2 7JP
Tel +44 (0)20 3222 0034
http://lunaandcurious.com
Whimsical, poetic collection of womenswear and home ornaments.

Mouki Mou
29 Chiltern Street, W1U 7PL
Tel +44 (0)20 7224 4010
www.moukimou.com
Elegant, stylish womenswear and accessories.

Roullier & White
125 Lordship Lane, East Dulwich, SE22 8HU
Tel +44 (0)20 8698 5150
www.roullierwhite.com
A fine selection of products to indulge in.

Solid ID
http://solidid.co.uk
Quintessentially British homewares.

The Garden Edit
http://thegardenedit.com
Contemporary selection of garden-related objects.

New York
ABC Home
888 & 881 Broadway at East 19th Street, NY 10003
Tel +1 (212) 473 3000
www.abchome.com
The go-to place for exquisite, covetable homewares and decorative wonders.

De Vera
1 Crosby Street, NY 10013
Tel +1 (212) 625 0838
26 East 81st Street, NY 10028
Tel +1 (212) 288 2288
www.deveraobjects.com
A finely curated selection of antiques and exquisite, luxurious curiosities.

The Future Perfect
55 Great Jones Street, NY 10012
Tel +1 (212) 473 2500
www.thefutureperfect.com
Also at 3085 Sacramento Street, San Francisco, CA 94115
Tel +1 (415) 932 6508
As they put it: 'Showcases for exceptional decorative arts and design.'

This is Story
144 10th Ave. at 19th Street, NY 10011
Tel +1 (212) 242 4853
http://thisisstory.com
'A retail concept that takes the point of view of a magazine.'

Osaka
ARTCOURT Gallery
www.artcourtgallery.com
A fantastic commercial gallery that exhibits up-and-coming young Japanese artists as well as established names.

Graf Shop and Kitchen
4-1-9 Nakanoshima, Kita-ku, Osaka-shi
Tel +81 (0)6 6459 2100
www.graf-d3.com
We could live in this shop and café!

Paris
107RIVOLI (the boutique at the Musée des Arts Décoratifs)
107 rue de Rivoli, 75001
Tel +33 (0)1 42 60 64 94
www.lesartsdecoratifs.fr
A great resource for unique creations, design books and a strong selection of ceramic and glass wares.

7L
7 rue de Lille, 75007
Tel +33 (0)1 42 92 03 58
www.librairie71.com
No wonder this selection of books on art, lifestyle, photography and design is so amazing: the maestro behind the venture is Karl Lagerfeld.

Affinité Terre
13 rue des Récollets, 75010
Tel +33 (0)1 43 80 01 24
www.affinite-terre.fr
Ceramicist Emmanuelle Wittmann presents her own work as well as that of other talents in her lovely gallery space.

Arty Dandy
www.artydandy.com
Several shops across Paris
As their slogan says: 'Remarkable products for remarkable people!'

Astier de Villatte
173 rue Saint-Honoré, 75001
Tel +33 (0)1 42 60 74 13
www.astierdevillatte.com
Own-brand ceramic tableware collection, with a few extra wonders specially curated for this shop.

Atelier Beau Travail
67 rue de la Mare, 75020
www.beautravail.fr
A collective of designers working in various media, creating fun and modern wares for the self and the home.

Bonbon au Palais
19 rue Monge, 75005
Tel +33 (0)1 78 56 15 72
www.bonbonsaupalais.fr
For those with a sweet tooth, an inner child or a wish to go down memory lane: traditional sweets from all over France.

Centre Commercial
2 rue de Marseille, 75010
Tel +33 (0)1 42 02 26 08
www.centrecommercial.cc
Concept store of the future: desirable fashion labels, vintage objects and eco-friendly Brazilian footwear/ accessory brand, Veja.

French Touche
1 rue Jacquemont, 75017
Tel +33 (0)1 42 63 31 36
www.frenchtouche.com
The anti-mass-retail-chain concept: unique, whimsical treats by independent designers in fashion, stationery, jewelry and homewares – nothing is overexposed.

Gallery S. Bensimon
111 rue de Turenne, 75003
Tel +33 (0)1 42 74 50 77
www.gallerybensimon.com
Desirable products from independent designers.

HOD
104 rue Vieille du Temple, 75003
Tel +33 (0)9 53 15 83 34
http://hod-boutique.com
The cream of the crop of today's jewelry and accessory designers.

L'Adorable Cabinet de Curiosités de Monsieur Honoré
30 rue de Charonne, 75011
Tel +33 (0)1 43 38 81 16
http://monsieur-honore.com
To create interiors fit for anthropologists or explorers.

La Cocotte
5 rue Paul Bert, 75011
Tel +33 (0)9 54 73 17 77
www.lacocotte.net
Amateur cooks and food lovers will love all things La Cocotte.

Les Curieuses
4 rue Oberkampf, 75011
Tel +33 (0)1 47 00 97 65
www.lescurieuses.com
Rare objects and unique furniture.

Miller et Bertaux
17 rue Ferdinand Duval, 75004
Tel +33 (0)1 42 78 28 39
www.milleretbertaux.com
Alongside own-label womenswear, candles and fragrances is a fantastic selection of out-of-the-ordinary objects.

Octagone
16 Place Vendôme, 75001
Tel +33 (0)6 70 58 65 33
http://octagone.fr
Contemporary arts and crafts in the heart of Paris, by appointment only.

Ostentatoire
101 rue de Turenne, 75003
Tel +33 (0)1 42 74 53 03
www.ostentatoire-paris.com
The best selection of up-and-coming fancy jewelry designers.

Papier Tigre
5 rue des Filles du Calvaire, 75003
www.papiertigre.fr
'Smart products to render everyday life more beautiful,' they say.

Rue Hérold
8 rue Hérold, 75001
Tel +33 (0)1 42 33 66 56
www.rueherold.com
Quality furnishing and clothing fabrics by the metre, at affordable prices, in a superbly stylish environment.

Sept Cinq
54 rue Notre Dame de Lorette, 75009
Tel +33 (0)9 83 55 05 95
www.sept-cinq.com
Accessories and fashion, 100% made in Paris!

Shang Xia
www.shang-xia.com
'Where contemporary design meets
Chinese heritage crafts.'

The Collection
33 rue de Poitou, 75003
Tel +33 (0)1 42 77 04 20
www.thecollection.fr
Contemporary homewares for your
walls and floors.

Sydney
Koskela (showroom and shop)
1/85 Dunning Ave., Rosebery, NSW 2018
Tel +61 (0)2 9280 0999
www.koskela.com.au
A homage to Australian craft: furniture,
homewares, books, all selected with flair.

Planet Furniture
114 Commonwealth Street, Surry Hills,
NSW 2010
Tel +61 (0)2 9211 5959
www.planetfurniture.com.au
Stylish hardwood furniture, but above
all a beautiful selection of contemporary
ceramic pieces.

Relax Home
instagram.com/relax_home
Well curated homewares and objects
regularly presented in pop-up shops.

The Minimalist
11 Albion Street, Surry Hills, NSW 2010
Tel +61 (0)2 9212 2622
www.theminimalist.com.au
Treasure trove of objects by young
contemporary designers.

Tokyo
Archivando
Kamiyama-cho 41-5 b1f, Shibuya,
150-0047
Tel +81 (0)3 5738 7253
www.archivando.jp
A fine selection of simple but fantastic
homewares.

Arts & Science
www.arts-science.com
Several shops around Tokyo and one
outpost in Paris: drop-dead gorgeous
fashion, accessories and rare objects.

Kio55
Tomigaya 1-9-19, Shibuya, 151-0063
Tel +81 (0)3 6804 9888
www.kio55.com
Little shop with pitch-perfect selection of
mostly tablewares (ceramics to die for).

Pivoine
Tomigaya 1-19-3, Shibuya
Tel +81 (0)3 3465 1193

http://puhura.co.jp
Delicate cornucopia of women's and
children's fashion and accessories.

Spiral Market
5-6-23 Minami Aoyama, Minato, 107-0062
Tel +81 (0)3 3498 5792
www.spiral.co.jp
International selection of utilitarian but
gorgeous design pieces: baby, home and
tablewares, jewelry, stationery, accessories.

UGUiSU The Little Shoppe
www.uguisulittleshoppe.com
Nestled in a leafy lane, a whimsical
selection of accessories, stationery
and more, curated by a lovely, English-
speaking owner.

Recommended websites & blogs

Some great resources for daydreaming
while browsing:

http://bloesem.blogs.com/bloesem
www.designspongeonline.com
http://dossier37.tumblr.com
www.finelittleday.com
www.henryhudson.com.au
www.ignant.de
www.notcot.org
www.poppytalk.com
http://samarrainelafee.blogspot.com
http://studiofludd.blogspot.com
www.supermarketsarah.com
www.theartfuldesperado.com
www.theplanthunter.com.au

Abigail Brown
www.facebook.com/pages/
Abigail-Brown-Textile-Artist-wwwabigail-
browncouk/198152930229402
http://instagram.com/abigailb81

Amy Jayne Hughes
https://twitter.com/AmyJayneHughes

Ana Hagopian
www.anahagopian.com

Anne Léger
www.facebook.com/anne.leger.96

Aude Tahon
www.facebook.com/aude.tahon

Bee Kingdom
www.facebook.com/beekingdomglass
http://instagram.com/beekingdomglass
www.pinterest.com/beekingdomglass
https://twitter.com/BeeKingdomGlass

Ben Fiess
www.flickr.com/photos/bfiess
http://instagram.com/bfiess

Bethamy Linton
www.facebook.com/pages/Bethamy-
Linton-Silversmith/621388624560860
http://instagram.com/bethamylinton

Brothers Dressler
www.facebook.com/pages/Brothers-
Dressler/134209793258314
http://instagram.com/brothersdressler
www.pinterest.com/brosdressler
https://twitter.com/BrosDressler

Catarina Riccabona
www.facebook.com/catarinariccabona
textiles
https://twitter.com/catariccabona

Cathy Miles
https://twitter.com/CathyMetalMiles

Claydies
http://instagram.com/claydies

Clémentine Dupré
www.facebook.com/dupreclem

Content & Container
www.facebook.com/contentandcontainer

Diana Fayt
http://dianafayt.blogspot.com
www.facebook.com/dianafaytceramics
http://www.flickr.com/photos/dianafayt
http://instagram.com/dianafayt
www.pinterest.com/dianafayt
https://twitter.com/dianafayt

Domenica More Gordon
http://instagram.com/Domenica
moregordon
https://twitter.com/DMoreGordon

Emmanuelle Dupont
www.facebook.com/emmanuelle.
dupont.773

Greg Hatton
www.flickr.com/photos/greghatton
http://greghatton.wordpress.com
http://instagram.com/greghatton

Hannah Waldron
www.facebook.com/hannahwaldrontextiles
http://hannahwaldron.blogspot.com
http://hannah-waldron.tumblr.com
https://twitter.com/hannahwaldron

Hanne Enemark
www.facebook.com/pages/Manifold/
118841604855654studiomanifold.org
https://twitter.com/studiomanifold

Iida-Kasaten
www.iida-kasaten.jp

Jennifer Collier
www.facebook.com/jennifer.collier.77
https://twitter.com/paperjennifer

Jeremy Maxwell Wintrebert
www.facebook.com/jeremy.wintrebert
http://instagram.com/jeremy_maxwell_
wintrebert

Jevda
www.etsy.com/shop/Jevda
www.facebook.com/jevda.jevda

Jude Miller
www.judemiller.com

Karen Barbé
http://blog.karenbarbe.com
www.facebook.com/karenbarbe.textileria

Katharine Morling
www.facebook.com/Katharine.Morlings.Studio
www.pinterest.com/katharine100

Ladies & Gentlemen Studio
www.facebook.com/jhclee
http://instagram.com/jeanlgstudio
www.pinterest.com/ladiesgentlemen

Leo Capote
http://instagram.com/leocapote

Lise Meunier
www.facebook.com/lise.meunier.547

Maartje van den Noort
www.facebook.com/maartje.vandnoort
www.pinterest.com/maartjetekent

Maïssa Toulet
www.facebook.com/pages/Maïssa-
Toulet/195434227166704

Manuela Castro Martins
www.facebook.com/manuela.c.martins.7

Margit Seland
www.facebook.com/margitselandcom

Matthias Kaiser
www.facebook.com/matthias.kaiser.756

Maxime Leroy
www.m-marceau.com

Michaël Cailloux
www.facebook.com/pages/Michaël-
Cailloux/1401084313462661
https://twitter.com/MichaelCailloux

Picture Credits

Miga de Pan
www.facebook.com/soymigadepan
www.pinterest.com/adrianamtorres

Mister Finch
www.etsy.com/shop/MisterFinch
www.facebook.com/MisterFinchTextileArt
www.flickr.com/photos/ohmisterfinch
http://mynameisfinch.blogspot.com
www.pinterest.com/mrfinchart

Naomi Paul
www.facebook.com/pages/
Naomi-Paul/100374600125518
https://twitter.com/naomipaul

Nyholm Cantrell
www.flickr.com/photos/appaz/
sets/72157632268638965
http://nyholmcantrell.blogspot.com

Oferenda Objetos
www.facebook.com/pages/Oferenda-
Objetos/125194937505542
http://instagram.com/oferendaobjetos
www.pinterest.com/oferenda

Paper-Cut-Project
www.facebook.com/pages/paper-cut-
project/240883772252
www.pinterest.com/biggik/paper-cut-
project
Facebook for Nikki Nye:
www.facebook.com/pages/The-Visual-
Beast/1386343301586309
Instagram for Nikki Nye:
http://instagram.com/biggik
Alternative site for Nikki Nye:
http://thevisualbeast.com
Twitter for Amy Flurry:
https://twitter.com/AmyFlurry

Papier à Êtres
www.facebook.com/pages/Papier-à-
êtres/1431940993703126

Polly Burton
www.pollyburton.co.uk

Renata Meirelles
www.flickr.com/photos/renatameirelles

Res Anima
www.resanima.de

Rosemary Milner
http://instagram.com/rosemarymilner
https://twitter.com/rosemarymilner

Sally Nencini
www.etsy.com/au/shop/SallyNencini
www.facebook.com/pages/Sally-
Nencini/344315869004015
www.pinterest.com/sallynencini
http://sallynencini.blogspot.com
https://twitter.com/sallynencini

Savo&Pomelina
www.facebook.com/pages/
Savopomelina/210346898987204

Sebastian Cox
www.facebook.com/sebastiancoxfurniture
www.flickr.com/photos/sebastiancox
www.pinterest.com/sebcox
https://twitter.com/sebcoxfurniture

Suna Fujita
www.facebook.com/sunafujita.shohei.
chisato

Susan Hipgrave
www.susanhipgrave.com

Takashi Tomii
www.facebook.com/takashi.tomii.9
http://instagram.com/takashitomii
http://konotami.blog.shinobi.jp

Tara Badcock
www.facebook.com/TaraBadcock
TextileArtist
www.flickr.com/photos/tarabadcock
http://teacosyrevolutiontara.blogspot.
com.au
https://twitter.com/TaraBadcock

Tara Shackell
www.facebook.com/tarashackellceramics
http://instagram.com/tarashackell
www.pinterest.com/tarashackell

Ulrika Berge
www.flickr.com/photos/ulrikaberge
http://vimeo.com/urikaberge

Vanilla Bicycles
www.facebook.com/sacha.white.94
www.flickr.com/photos/42587323@N08

Young-I Kim
www.youngikim.de

Zoé Ouvrier
www.facebook.com/zoe.ouvrier
www.pinterest.com/alexbennaim/zoe-ouvrier

p.1 Courtesy of Emmanuelle Dupont
(www.emmanuelle-dupont.com).

pp.2–3 Ester Segarra
(www.e-segarra.com).

Abigail Brown p.8 no. 1, p.11 nos
5 & 7 Emma Collins (www.eskimorose-
photography.com); p.8 no. 2, p.9 no. 3,
p.10 no. 4, p.11 no. 6, p.308 nos 1,
2, 3, 4 & 5 courtesy of Abigail Brown
(www.abigail-brown.co.uk).

Amy Jayne Hughes p.12 no. 1, p.13 no.
4, p.15 no. 7, p.256 no. 1 courtesy of
Amy Jayne Hughes (www.amyjaynehughes.
com); p.12 no. 2, p.13 no. 3, p.14 no.
5, p.256 no. 2 Ester Segarra (www.e-
segarra.com); p.15 no. 6 Joanne Underhill
(www.structuraleye.co.uk).

Ana Hagopian all photos by Fabián
Vázquez Savareikas (www.bytalking.com).

Anne Léger p.20 nos 1 & 2 Léo Léger
Martin; p.21 no. 3, p.23 no. 6 Kirsti
Reinsberg Mørch; p.22 no. 4, p.23 no. 5,
p.273 nos 6, 7 & 8 courtesy of Anne Léger
(www.anneleger.com).

Aude Tahon p.24 nos 1 & 2, p.25 no.
5 Caterina Suzzi (www.imagesensibles.
com); p.25 nos 3 & 4, p.26 nos 6 & 7,
p.27 no. 8, p.252 nos 1 & 2, p.277
no. 7 Hortense Vinet (www.hortensevinet.
net); p.277 nos 4, 5 & 6 Ricardo Abrahao
(www.ricardoabrahao.com/www.speos.fr)
& Vasily Veprintsev (www.veprintsev.com/
www.speos.fr).

Bee Kingdom all photos by Erin Wallace
(www.erinwallacephotography.com).

Ben Fiess all photos courtesy of Ben Fiess
(www.bfiess.com).

Bethamy Linton p.36 nos 1 & 2, p.38 no.
8, p.39 no. 11 Michelle Taylor (www.
fotomich.com.au); p.37 nos 3 & 4, p.38
nos 5, 6 & 7, p.39 nos 9 & 10, p.272
nos 1, 2, 3, 4 & 5, p.289 nos 6 & 7
Bewley George Shaylor.

Brothers Dressler p.40 no. 1, p.41 no.
3, pp.42–3 no. 6 Dylan Macleod; p.40
no. 2 Clay Stang (www.claystang.com);
p.42 nos 4 & 5, p.282 no. 2, p.266
no. 1 courtesy of Brothers Dressler (www.
brothersdressler.com); p.266 no. 2, p.282
no. 1 Janet Kimber (www.janetkimber.com).

Catarina Riccabona p.44 no. 1, p.45 nos
3 & 4, p.46 nos 6, 7 & 9, p.312 nos 3 &
4 courtesy of Catarina Riccabona (www.
catarinariccabona.com); p.44 no. 2, p.45
no. 5, p.46 no. 8, p.47 nos 10 & 11

Laura Adburgham (www.lauraadburgham.
com).

Cathy Miles p.48 nos 1 & 2, p.50 nos 5
& 6, p.291 no. 7 Graham Oakes (www.
oakesstudios.co.uk); p.49 no. 3, p.51 no.
7, p.291 nos 5 & 6 courtesy of Cathy Miles
(www.cathymiles.com); p.50 no. 4 Patrick
Dandy (www.patrickdandy.tumblr.com).

Claydies all photos by Morgan Morell
(www.morganmorell.com).

Clémentine Dupré all photos by Anthony
Girardi (www.anthonygirardi.com).

Content & Container p.60 no. 1, p.61 no.
3, p.63 no. 7, p.303 nos 5 & 6 Christian
Angl (www.christian-angl.de); p.60 no.
2, p.61 no. 4, p.62 no. 5, p.303 no.
4 Natalie Richter; p.62 no. 6, p.280
nos 1 & 2 Mareen Fischinger (www.
mareenfischinger.com).

Diana Fayt all photos by Alessandra Cave
(www.alessandracave.com).

Domenica More Gordon p.68 no. 1,
p.71 no. 7, p.251 nos 4, 5 & 6, p.320
Claire Lloyd (www.clairelloyd.com/www.
clairelloydloves.com); p.68 no. 2 (accessories
tailored by Diane Slater), p.69 no. 3, p.70
nos 4, 5 & 6 (clothes and accessories tailored
by Diane Slater) courtesy of Domenica More
Gordon (www.domenicamoregordon.com);
p.279 nos 5, 6, 7 & 8 courtesy of Arts &
Science (www.arts-science.com), photography
by Satoshi Yamaguchi.

Emmanuelle Dupont p.1, p.72 no. 1, p.74
no. 4, p.252 no. 3 courtesy of Emmanuelle
Dupont (www.emmanuelle-dupont.com);
p.72 no. 2, p.73 no. 3 Jennifer Ryan
(www.jennyryan.book.fr); p.75 no. 5 &
7 Anne-Lise Quesnel; p.75 no. 6 Louve
Delfieu (www.louvedelfieu.com).

Greg Hatton all photos by Shantanu
Starick (www.shantanustarick.com/
www.thepixelproject.com).

Hannah Waldron all photos courtesy of
Hannah Waldron (www.hannahwaldron.
co.uk), except for p.82 no. 5 by Martin
Holtkamp (http://ma-ho.com) for Link
(http://thelinkcollective.com).

Hanne Enemark pp.2–3, p.84 no. 2, p.85
nos 4 & 5, p.86 no. 7, p.87 no. 9, p.269
nos 4, 5 & 6, p.285 no. 6, Ester Segarra
(www.e-segarra.com); p.84 no. 1, p.85
no. 3, p.86 nos 6 & 8 Nicola Tree (www.
nicolatree.com).

Iida-Kasaten p.88 no. 1, p.89 no. 5,
p.91 nos 9 & 11, p.278 nos 1 & 2

courtesy of Iida Kasaten Textile (www.iida-kasaten.jp); p.88 no. 2, p.89 nos 3 & 4, p.90 nos 6 & 7, p.91 no. 10 Shuhei Tonami (http://tonami-s.com); p.90 no. 8 Shuhei Tonami (http://tonami-s.com) for *The Design of IIDA KASATEN*, published by PIE International (www.pie.co.jp).

Jennifer Collier p.92 nos 1 & 2, p.93 nos 3 & 4, p.94 no. 6, pp.94–5 no. 8 Luke Richardson (www.lukerichardsonphotography.com); p.93 no. 5, p.294 no. 4 Luke Unsworth (www.lukeunsworth.co.uk); p.94 no. 7, p.294 nos 1, 2 & 3 Gareth Perry.

Jeremy Maxwell Wintrebert p.96 no. 1, p.97 nos 3 & 4, p.98 no. 6, 7 & 8 Laurent Vilain; p.96 no. 2, p.97 no. 5, p.99 no. 9, p.286 no. 1 courtesy of Jeremy Maxwell Wintrebert (www.jeremyglass.com); p.286 no. 2 Petr Krejci (www.petrkrejci.com).

Jevda all photos courtesy of Jenny Eve van den Arend (http://jevda.blogspot.com).

Jude Miller all photos courtesy of Jude Miller (www.judemiller.com), except for p.104 no. 1 Wendy Sheffield and p.293 no. 3 Stephen Jones.

Karen Barbé all photos courtesy of Karen Barbé (www.karenbarbe.com).

Katharine Morling p.112 no. 1, p.115 nos 7 & 8, p.257 nos 3, 5 & 6 Stephen Brayne (www.stephenbrayne.com); p.112 no. 2, p.113 nos 4 & 5, p.114 no. 6 photographer Paul Dixon (www.pauldixonpictures.co.uk) & stylist Marlies Winkelmeier (www.marlieswinkelmeier.com); p.113 no. 3, p.257 no. 4 Jeremy Johns (www.jeremyjohns.co.uk).

Ladies & Gentlemen Studio p.116 no. 1, p.119 nos 8 & 9, p.261 no. 2 Charlie Schuck (www.charlieschuck.com); p.116 no. 2, p.117 nos 3, 4, 5 & 6, p.118 no. 7, p.261 no. 3, pp.282–83 no. 5, p.313 nos 5, 6 & 7 courtesy of Ladies & Gentlemen Studio (www.ladiesandgentlemenstudio.com).

Leo Capote all photos by Marcelo Stefanovicz (www.stefanovicz.com).

Lise Meunier all photos courtesy of Lise Meunier (http://lise-meunier.blogspot.com).

Maartje van den Noort p.128 nos 1 & 2, p.129 no. 4, p.131 nos 7, 8 & 9, p.314 nos 1 & 2 courtesy of Maartje van den Noort (www.maartjevandennoort.nl); p.129 no. 3, p.130 nos 5 & 6 Anneke Hymmen (www.annekehymmen.nl); p.314 nos 3 & 4 Eveline Maat (www.evelinemaat.nl).

Maïssa Toulet p.132 no. 1, p.134 nos 5 & 6 Laurent Deglicourt (http://les.beaux.jours.over-blog.com); p.132 no. 2, p.134 no. 4, p.248 no. 2 Cécile Hug (http://cecilehug.blogspot.fr); p.133 no. 3 courtesy of Maïssa Toulet (www.maissatoulet.fr); p.135 no. 7, p.248 nos 1 & 3 Ludovic Bollo (www.ludovicbollo.com).

Manuela Castro Martins all photos by Abílio Cardoso (abiliofotografo@gmail.com).

Margit Seland all photos courtesy of Margit Seland (www.margitseland.com), except for p.140 no. 1 Caroline Coehorst (www.carolinecoehorst.nl).

Matthias Kaiser p.144 no. 1, p.145 no. 3, p.146 nos 5 & 6, p.147 nos 7, 8, 9 & 10, p.258 nos 1, 2, 3, 4 & 5, p.301 nos 5, 6, 7, 8 & 9 Jens Preusse (www.lotsen.at); p.144 no. 2, p.146 no. 4 Michael Turkiewicz (www.designandart.at).

Maxime Leroy all photos by Marjorie Hasley.

Michaël Cailloux p.152 nos 1 & 2, p.153 no. 3, p.154 nos 6 & 7 Camille de Laurens (www.camilledelaurens.com); p.153 no. 4, p.253 no. 6 Marc Noël; p.153 no. 5, p.253 nos 4, 5 & 7 Gilles Hirgorom; p.155 no. 8, p.281 nos 5, 6 & 7, p.292 no. 1 courtesy of Michaël Cailloux (www.michaelcailloux.com).

Miga de Pan all photos courtesy of Adriana Torres (www.migadepan.com.ar), except for p.156 no. 2 Rodrigo Gorosterrazú.

Mister Finch all photos courtesy of Mister Finch (www.mister-finch.com).

Naomi Paul p.164 no. 1, p.165 nos 3 & 5 courtesy of Naomi Paul (www.naomipaul.co.uk); p.164 no. 2, p.165 no. 4, p.166 no. 6, p.167 no. 7, p.287 nos 3, 4, 5 & 6 Nick Rochowski Photography (www.rochowski.net).

Nyholm Cantrell p.168 no. 1, p.169 no. 3, p.170 nos 6 & 8 Poul Nyholm (www.poulnyholm.dk); p.168 no. 2, p.169 nos 4 & 5, p.171 no. 9, p.270 nos 2 & 3 courtesy of Karen Nyholm (www.nyholmcantrell.dk); p.170 no. 7, p.171 no. 10, p.270 nos 1 & 4 courtesy of Ned Cantrell (www.nyholmcantrell.dk).

Oferenda Objetos p.172 nos 1 & 2, p.173 nos 3, 4 & 5, p.174 nos 6 & 8, p.175 no. 9, p.263 nos 4, 5, 6 & 7 Marcelo Donadussi (www.mdonadussi.com.br); p.174 no. 7 Mariana Chama.

Paper-Cut-Project p.176 nos 1 & 2, p.177 no. 4, p.178 nos 6 & 7 Rinne Allen (www.rinneallen.com); p.177 no. 3, p.178 no. 5, p.179 no. 8, p.295 nos 5, 6, 7 & 8 courtesy of Amy Flurry and Nikki Rye (www.paper-cut-project.com).

Papier à Êtres all photos by Fabrice Besse (www.cactusstudio.fr).

Polly Burton all photos by Millie Burton (www.millieburton.com), except for p.187 no. 5 Neri Kamcili (www.nerikamcili.com).

Renata Meirelles p.188 no. 1, p.189 nos 3 & 4, p.190 nos 6, 7 & 8, p.191 nos 9 & 10, p.275 nos 3, 4 & 5 Ligia Eça Negreiros (www.flickr.com/photos/ligia-negreiros); p.188 no. 2, p.189 no. 5 Cristina Guimarães.

Res Anima p.192 no. 1, p.193 no. 3, p.195 no. 6, p.262 nos 1 & 3 Philip Kottlorz (www.philipkottlorz.com); p.192 no. 2, p.194 nos 4 & 5, p.195 nos 7 & 8, p.262 no. 2 courtesy of Philipp Hinderer (www.resanima.de).

Rosemary Milner all photos by Ian Edward Prentice (www.ianep.co.uk).

Sally Nencini p.200 no. 1, p.202 nos 6 & 8 Thea Courtney (www.theacourtneyphotography.com); p.200 no. 2, p.201 nos 3, 4 & 5 Sara Lloyd (www.saralloyd.co.uk); p.202 no. 7, p.203 nos 9 & 10, p.311 nos 4, 5, 6, 7 & 8 courtesy of Sally Nencini (www.sallynencini.com); p.305 nos 4, 5 & 6 courtesy of Peter Nencini (www.peternencini.co.uk).

Savo&Pomelina all photos courtesy of Eva Craenhals (www.savopomelina.be).

Sebastian Cox all images by Spadge UK (www.spadgeuk.com).

Suna Fujita all photos courtesy of fujita + chisato (http://blog.goo.ne.jp/fujitachisato).

Susan Hipgrave all photos by Craig Wall (www.craigwall.com.au).

Takashi Tomii all photos courtesy of Takashi Tomii (www.takashitomii.com).

Tara Badcock p.224 nos 1 & 2, p.227 no. 5 Claire Badcock; p.225 no. 3, p.227 nos 6 & 7, p.315 nos 8, 9 & 10 courtesy of Tara Badcock (www.tarabadcock.com); p.226 no. 4 Monique Germon (www.moniquegermon.com).

Tara Shackell p.228 no. 1, p.229 nos 3, 4 & 5, p.230 nos 6 & 8, p.297 nos 5, 6 & 7 courtesy of Tara Shackell (www.tarashackell.com); p.228 no. 2 Eve Wilson (www.evewilson.com.au); p.230 no. 7, p.231 no. 9 Eve Wilson (www.evewilson.com.au), styled by Paige Anderson.

Ulrika Berge p.232 no. 1, p.233 no. 3, p.235 nos 7 & 8 Jenny Simm (http://mennej.tumblr.com); p.232 no. 2, p.233 nos 4 & 5, pp.234–35 no. 6, p.250 nos 1, 2 & 3 courtesy of Ulrika Berge (www.ulrikaberge.se).

Vanilla Bicycles p.236 no. 1 Jeff Curtes (www.jeffcurtes.com); p.236 no. 2, p.237 no. 3, p.238 no. 6, p.239 no. 7, p.290 nos 1, 2, 3 & 4 Bob Huff (www.bobhuffphoto.com); p.238 nos 4 & 5, p.239 no. 8 Michael Tabtabai (www.leaveitontheroad.com).

Young-I Kim p.240 nos 1 & 2, p.241 nos 4 & 5, p.242 nos 6 & 7, p.243 nos 8 & 9 Bernhard Simon; p.241 no. 3, p.242 nos 10 & 11, p.243 nos 12 & 13, p.288 nos 1, 2, 3, 4 & 5 courtesy of Young-I Kim (www.youngikim.de).

Zoé Ouvrier p.244 no. 1, p.245 no. 3 Philip Provily (www.philipprovily.com); p.244 no. 2 Chris Tubbs (www.christubbsphotography.com); p.245 no. 4 Arik Levy (www.ariklevy.fr); p.245 no. 5, p.265 nos 6 & 8 Florian Kleinefenn (www.kleinefenn.com); p.246 no. 6 Thierry Depagne/courtesy of India Mahdavi; p.247 no. 7 Petr Krejci (www.petrkrejci.com); p.265 no. 7 Ian Scigliuzzi (www.scigliuzzi.com).

p.320 A little dog handmade in felt by Domenica More Gordon for Arts & Science's Tokyo exhibition, 'Show Dogs'. Photo courtesy of Arts & Science (www.arts-science.com), photography by Satoshi Yamaguchi.

...nowledgments

I would like to offer a big round of applause to all the participants who wholeheartedly embraced this project: the photographers whose generosity has allowed the book to exist; the friends and colleagues who made suggestions, assisted, collaborated on and supported the book, in particular Michiko Kiyosawa of ARTCOURT Gallery in Osaka and the team behind Arts & Science in Tokyo. A big thank you also to my publisher, Thames & Hudson, and to the designer of this book's beautiful pages, Myfanwy Vernon-Hunt of This-Side Studio.

Above all, the book is dedicated to all those who are making a positive difference in the world today. It cannot be stressed enough that artisans, by making objects with love – and an ever-growing number of their supporters, by purchasing them – are slowly but surely reversing the trend of generic mass-consumption. Let us all put our party hats on. It is time to celebrate!

About the Author

Olivier Dupon is an expert in the fields of lifestyle and fashion. He began his career at Christian Dior, then worked as a buyer and project manager for several large retail companies before running his own boutique in Australia for several years. Now based in London, he scouts international markets in search of exciting new practitioners of design/art/craft. His previous books include *The New Artisans* (2011), *The New Jewelers* (2012), *The New Pâtissiers* (2013) and *Floral Contemporary* (2014), all published by Thames & Hudson. His new book on shoes will be published in 2015.